GLUTEN FREE WORLD TOUR COOKBOOK

INTERNATIONALLY INSPIRED GLUTEN FREE RECIPES

Katie Moseman

To Jason with love

Table of Contents

Introduction

Why is this book called *Gluten Free World Tour Cookbook*?

Most conversations with my mother start with "Whatcha fixin' for dinner?" Sometimes I ask her; sometimes she asks me.

When we ask one another this question, we're not asking for a report that covers "Just the facts, ma'am." The real question—if you read between the lines—is this: *Have you come up with any new cooking ideas lately?*

A taste of something different and exciting isn't just a source of sustenance; it's a symbolic escape from the everyday confines of the kitchen. No matter where you're from, the *Gluten Free World Tour Cookbook* is designed to be an adventure to somewhere new.

How is this cookbook different?

When found out I could no longer eat gluten, I started converting the most familiar and simple recipes in my repertoire from gluten-filled to gluten free. After a while, I got tired of the same old, same old. I needed to feel like I wasn't confined by my dietary restriction, so I started exploring recipe ideas I'd never tried before: gluten free, but packed with ideas and flavors that were new to me.

With *Gluten Free World Tour Cookbook* in hand, you'll have your own travel guide to cuisines around the world. You're about to discover a whole world of gluten free deliciousness.

How is this book organized?

The gluten free world tour kicks off with *Starters and Sides*, like Cauliflower Falafel with Tahini Drizzle, continues into *Main Dishes* (divided into *Handheld* goodness like Cuban Sandwich Sliders and *Knife and Fork* crowd-pleasers like Beef Stifado), and wraps up with a bevy of *Desserts* like Rice Cream with Cherry Sauce.

Many recipes include a helpful sidebar to help you *Know Your Ingredients*, or explore recipe methods and variations with a *Technique Takeaway*.

After you've enjoyed all the recipes, you'll find more than a dozen *Recommended Reading* cookbook suggestions so you can keep on traveling around the world, one recipe at a time!

An Important Note About Ingredients

Ingredient Safety

Some follow a gluten free diet by choice; others follow a gluten free diet due to gluten intolerance or celiac disease. Some individuals are more sensitive to gluten contamination than others. Every individual is different.

In this cookbook, recipe ingredient lists will specifically call for flour, bread, and pasta that is gluten free. Other ingredients, such as spices, condiments, sauces, meat, fruit, cheese, and vegetables—to name a few—are not (in most cases) specifically described as gluten free in the ingredient lists, to avoid the redundancy of repeating "gluten free" over and over.

If you are following a gluten free diet for health reasons, please check with the manufacturer or producer of any given ingredient to ensure that it meets your needs. Remember, this cookbook is not intended as a substitute for the medical advice of a doctor. Consult a physician for all health matters, and for any symptoms that may require diagnosis or medical attention.

Gluten Free Flour Options

The majority of the recipes that call for a gluten free flour blend have been tested with several widely available gluten free flour blends, such as Cup4Cup Multipurpose Flour or Bob's Red Mill Gluten Free 1-to-1 Baking Flour. Several recipes call for a specific flour in the ingredient list, due to its superior performance in that particular recipe. Always use your own judgment regarding which gluten free flours or blends are suitable for your dietary requirements.

Starters & Sides

Cauliflower Falafel with Tahini Drizzle

Recipe contributed by Liz Alvarez – founder, writer and wildly creative cook at BuildingOurRez.com

Traditional Middle Eastern falafel is made with chickpeas, but this version changes it up by replacing chickpeas with cauliflower. Piled high on a lettuce wrap, drizzled with sauce, and garnished with fresh cucumber and tomato salad, falafel works great as a snack or a meal.

Prep Time: 10 minutes
Cook Time: 20 minutes
Total Time: 30 minutes
Yield: 6 servings,
or approximately 2 dozen pieces

For the cucumber and tomato salad:
8 ounces cherry tomatoes
(or substitute 1 to 2 regular
 tomatoes)
1 cucumber
1 tablespoon lemon juice
2 cloves garlic
1 head of leaf lettuce

For the tahini sauce:
¾ cup tahini
2 whole carrots
Zest of one lemon
¼ cup lemon juice
4 cloves garlic
1 teaspoon crushed red pepper
1 cup water

For the falafel:
1 head of cauliflower
1 onion, peeled and chopped
1 bunch cilantro (about 2 cups loosely packed, before chopping)
1 bunch parsley (about 2 cups loosely packed, before chopping)
8 cloves garlic, peeled
2 teaspoons cumin
2 teaspoons coriander
1 teaspoon salt
2 teaspoons paprika
1/2 teaspoon crushed red pepper
1 tablespoon lemon juice
2 eggs
1 cup arrowroot powder
2 cups almond flour
1 teaspoon baking powder
About 2 cups oil, for frying

For the cucumber and tomato salad:

1. Chop the tomatoes and cucumber into approximately ½ inch pieces. Add to a small bowl and stir in garlic and lemon juice. Toss to coat. Set aside.

For the tahini sauce:

1. Chop carrots into 1 inch slices and add to a pot with enough water to cover the carrot slices. Bring the water to a boil and cook for about 10 minutes, or until very soft. (A fork should slide in easily.) Drain.

2. Add cooked carrots to a blender with tahini, lemon zest, juice, garlic and crushed red pepper. Blend until combined.

3. With the blender running, open the door on the lid and stream in the water until the sauce comes together and is a good consistency for drizzling. Remove to a bowl and set aside.

For the falafel:

1. Chop cauliflower into small florets. Add to a food processor and pulse until the pieces are the very finely minced and resemble rice. Remove to a mixing bowl.

2. Add all other falafel ingredients to the food processor except cauliflower, almond flour, arrowroot powder, baking powder and oil, and blend until thoroughly mixed. It should form a sauce. Add the cauliflower back into the food processor, and pulse until combined.

3. Remove the contents of the food processor to a bowl and stir in the almond flour, arrowroot powder, and baking powder.

4. Add oil about 1 to 2 inches deep in a skillet. Heat over medium-high heat until shimmering. Drop rounded tablespoons of falafel batter into the skillet, leaving a couple inches between each falafel; don't overcrowd the pan. Cook 1 to 3 minutes, or until you see the edges are getting browned, then flip the pieces of falafel. Cook 1 to 3 minutes on the second side. Remove with a slotted spoon to a plate lined with a paper towel to drain excess oil. Falafel are done when they turn from green to dark brown and golden.

5. To assemble, wash as many leaves of lettuce as you need, layering two pieces of lettuce together for each wrap (two pieces instead of one makes the wrap sturdier). Lay a few falafel in the middle of the lettuce, drizzle with tahini sauce, then add the cucumber salad on top or serve it on the side.

Elote (Mexican Grilled Corn)

Elote, a delightful Mexican version of corn on the cob, is sold by street vendors in Mexico. Elote means "corn on the cob" in Spanish. There are many variations on elote, but most include mayonnaise, ancho chile pepper, and cotija cheese (a fresh and crumbly cheese with a mild, nutty flavor).

Prep Time: 25 minutes
Cook Time: 20 minutes
Total Time: 45 minutes
Yield: 6 ears of corn

---

6 ears of corn, husks on
⅓ cup mayonnaise
2 tablespoons sour cream
½ teaspoon ground ancho chile pepper, plus more for serving
2 teaspoons fresh lime juice
Pinch of salt
1 cup cotija cheese crumbles
Lime wedges for serving

1. Peel back the husks to loosen them from the corn. Do not remove husks. Soak the corn in cold water for 20 minutes.
2. Prepare a medium hot grill (about 350°F).
3. Peel back the husks leaving at least two outer layers attached at the end. Remove the silk and pull the husks back up. Tie with cooking twine or a piece of husk (not too tightly so that steam can be released during grilling).
4. Place the ears on the grill. Cover grill. Cook for 20 minutes, turning ears every 5 minutes for even cooking. The corn is done when the kernels are soft. Be careful not to overcook or the corn will be mushy.
5. While the ears are grilling, make the spread. In a small bowl, add mayonnaise, sour cream, ancho chile pepper, lime juice, and salt. Stir to combine.
6. Spread a thin layer of the cheese on a plate or sheet of aluminum foil.
7. Handle the grilled corn with caution because they will be hot. Safety first to avoid burns.
8. Peel back and remove the husk from an ear of corn. Brush the spread on the corn. Roll the coated corn in the cheese. Repeat process with remaining corn.
9. Serve immediately with additional ancho chile pepper and lime wedges. Squeeze the lime over the corn and sprinkle with more pepper if desired.

Ancho Chile Peppers

Ancho chile peppers are poblano peppers that have been allowed to ripen before being dried. When whole, they are dark red with a very wrinkled appearance, but they're also sold pre-ground as ancho chile pepper powder, making them easy to add to recipes or as a garnish. They add mild heat with a touch of natural sweetness.

Cotija Cheese

There are many delicious varieties of Mexican cheese. Cotija cheese, named after the town of Cotija in Mexico, is an salty, aged, crumbly cheese made from cow's milk. It's used as a garnish much like Parmesan cheese is used in Italian cuisine.

Know Your Ingredients

Champiñones al Ajillo (Garlic Mushrooms)

Champiñones al ajillo is Spanish for "garlic mushrooms." This classic tapas dish originated in Spain and can be served alongside other appetizers or as an accompaniment to a main course.

Prep Time: 5 minutes
Cook Time: 5 minutes
Total Time: 10 minutes
Yield: 4 servings

3 tablespoons extra virgin olive oil
10 large button mushrooms
5 cloves garlic, peeled
1 tablespoon lemon juice
2 tablespoons dry sherry,
    or cooking sherry
¼ teaspoon smoked paprika
½ teaspoon red pepper flakes
A few strands of saffron
½ tablespoon fresh chopped parsley
Salt and pepper to taste
Toasted gluten free bread,
    for serving

1. Cut mushrooms into quarters and mince the garlic.
2. Heat the olive oil in a saute pan over medium heat. Add mushrooms and saute for a few minutes. Add minced garlic, lemon juice, sherry, smoked paprika, and red pepper flakes. Cook for 5 minutes, stirring often.
3. Remove pan from heat and stir in the saffron and parsley. Taste, and add salt and pepper as desired.
4. Serve hot with toasted bread.

Recipe contributed by SpicesInc.com.

Saffron

Saffron is the world's expensive spice. When measured by the pound, saffron's retail price is in the thousands of dollars. Luckily, most recipes only call for a strand or two in order to harness its unique flavor and beautiful color. Be careful to purchase whole saffron strands rather than pre-ground; pre-ground saffron is more likely to be adulterated with other, cheaper ingredients.

Sherry

Sherry is a type of fortified wine from Spain. "Fortified" means that extra spirits are added to the wine after fermentation to increase the alcohol content. Some sherries are sweet, while others are not. A sherry that is not sweet is described as dry sherry.

Know Your Ingredients

_____

_____

_____

_____

_____

Dodo (Nigerian Fried Plantains)

Fried plantains are popular around the world. Each plantain-growing region has its own unique recipe for frying plantains, which can include variations on the ripeness of the plantain, the method of cutting the plantain flesh, the flavorings used, and the type of cooking oil. This version from Nigeria uses ripe plantains cut into elongated slices, fried in oil, and seasoned with salt.

Prep Time: 5 minutes
Cook Time: 8 minutes
Total Time: 13 minutes
Yield: 4 servings

Canola oil
2 ripe plantains (the skin on the
    plantains should be mostly black)
Salt

1. Peel the plantain. Cut diagonally across the plantain to create elongated slices about ½inch thick (they'll have tapering ends).
2. Add enough canola oil to a large frying pan for the oil to come ⅓ inch up the side of the pan. Preheat the pan with the oil in it over medium heat for a few minutes, until the oil is shimmering in appearance, and a tiny piece of plantain dropped in the oil sizzles.
3. Using tongs, carefully lay the slices of plantain into the hot oil. Do not overlap the slices or overcrowd the pan. Cook for 3 to 4 minutes, or until the slices are golden brown on one side, then flip and cook the other side of the slices for 3 to 4 minutes until that side is also golden brown.
4. Gently remove the slices from the pan and place on paper towels to drain. Sprinkle with salt and serve immediately.

Popped Sorghum

Sorghum is a grain that originated in Africa and spread to other countries around the world. In India, sorghum kernels are popped like popcorn for a tiny, tasty snack. Even with practice popping them, you'll find that not all the kernels will pop—but (unlike popcorn) you can eat the kernels anyway! They provide a nutty, crunchy contrast to the popped sorghum.

Prep Time: 0 minutes
Cook Time: 5 minutes
Total Time: 5 minutes
Yield: 1 serving

1. Add the ghee to a large, deep pot with a lid (a Dutch oven is ideal). Drop in 5 or 6 kernels of sorghum. Heat the pot, covered, over medium high heat for a few minutes until you hear the kernels start to pop.
2. Remove the lid, pour in the remaining kernels, and set the lid back on the pot slightly ajar so that steam can escape. Shake the pot back and forth gently to coat all the kernels and keep them moving to prevent burning.
3. When popping slows, remove the pot from the heat and remove the lid entirely. Carefully pour the popped and unpopped kernels into a bowl and toss with salt, if desired, to taste.

2 tablespoons ghee
    (or substitute canola oil if desired)
¼ cup gluten free whole grain
    sorghum kernels
Very fine salt, for topping

Three More Ways to Make Roasted Nuts

1. Swap in raw pecans, walnuts, or cashews to substitute for the cocktail peanuts.
2. Try substituting a different spice mix for the sriracha seasoning, such as chili powder or barbecue seasoning.
3. To serve a crowd, double the quantities and make the recipe ahead of time.

Sriracha Spiced Peanuts

Sriracha seasoning is a dry version of Thai sriracha sauce, which makes it useful for recipes that require a punch of flavor without adding extra liquid. These sweet and spicy peanuts are excellent for pairing with a crisp, cold beverage.

Prep Time: 5 minutes
Cook Time: 10 minutes
Total Time: 15 minutes
Yield: 2 cups

1. Preheat oven to 350°F.
2. Place peanuts in a medium bowl.
3. Stir together butter, sriracha seasoning, and brown sugar. Pour over peanuts and stir to coat.
4. Spread peanuts out in single layer on a rimmed baking sheet.
5. Bake for 10 minutes, stirring halfway through baking.
6. Cool to room temperature.

12 ounces lightly salted cocktail peanuts
1 ½ tablespoons unsalted butter, melted
1 teaspoon sriracha seasoning (not sriracha sauce)
1 teaspoon firmly packed brown sugar

Maple Glazed Cashews

The sweet sap of the maple tree makes an excellent coating for roasted nuts. Most of the world's maple syrup comes from Canada, while cashews are the fruit of the tropical cashew tree—making this nutty snack a fusion of flavors from around the globe.

Prep Time: 1 minute
Cook Time: 10 minutes
Total Time: 11 minutes
Yield: 4 servings

2 cups raw cashews
2 tablespoon maple syrup
Pinch of salt

1. Preheat oven to 350°F and line a baking sheet with parchment paper to prevent sticking.
2. In a mixing bowl, combine the ingredients and stir until the cashews are evenly coated.
3. Pour the mixture on the parchment paper and spread out the cashews. Bake for 10 minutes, until the cashews color slightly. Do not overcook; they will burn quickly.
4. Let cool until just barely warm, then serve. Or let cool completely and cover airtight to store.

Maple Syrup

Maple syrup is produced from the sap of the maple tree. Most of the pure maple syrup sold in grocery stores is considered Grade A maple syrup, which comes in four distinct varieties: Golden Color and Delicate Taste, Amber Color and Rich Taste, Dark Color and Robust Taste, Very Dark Color and Strong Taste.

For baking and roasting purposes, Amber Color and Rich Taste or Dark Color and Robust Taste typically work best. There's no hard-and-fast rule, though; feel free to choose any variety that suits your palate.

Know
Your
Ingredients

Hummus with Jalapeño Cilantro Relish

Hummus is a well-known Mediterranean food, but it pairs surprisingly well with flavors originating from Mexican cuisine. This hummus recipe combines smooth and creamy hummus with a vivid green topping made from chopped jalapeño and cilantro. It's an excellent party dip, or you can use it as a spread on sandwiches or wraps instead of mayonnaise.

Prep Time: 15 minutes
Inactive Time: 30 minutes
   (or more if desired)
Total Time: 45 minutes
Yield: 2 cups hummus

For the hummus:
15 ounces canned chickpeas
¼ cup tahini
2 tablespoons fresh lemon juice
1 clove garlic crushed
¼ teaspoon ground chipotle chile pepper powder
¾ teaspoon sea salt
½ teaspoon extra virgin olive oil, plus more for serving

For the relish:
1 fresh jalapeño, seeded and
   finely chopped
⅓ cup chopped fresh cilantro
Dash of salt
Squeeze of fresh lime

For the hummus:

1. Drain the canned chickpeas into a colander and rinse thoroughly.
2. Place the chickpeas in a food processor and process until you have a thick paste. Add the salt, tahini, lemon juice, garlic, and chipotle chile pepper powder, then process again. Scrape down the sides of the processor as necessary to ensure even blending. Drizzle in the ½ teaspoon of olive oil, then process again.
3. Taste the hummus to see if it has a very smooth texture. If not, process again until you do. Add water a tablespoon at a time, if need, and continue processing until totally smooth. Transfer the hummus to a storage container and press a sheet of plastic wrap directly onto the surface of the hummus to prevent it from forming a skin. Refrigerate for at least 30 minutes, but preferably for several hours to let the flavors develop.

For the relish:

1. When you are ready to serve the hummus, make the salsa garnish. Combine the chopped jalapeño, cilantro, dash of salt, and lime in a mortar or food processor. Grind or process until the jalapeño is in small pieces and the mixture is similar in texture to a thick pesto.

To serve:

1. Scoop the hummus into a bowl or serving dish. Put the relish in the center of the hummus. Use the back of a spoon to indent a moat in the shape of a circle around the center of the hummus. Pour olive oil into the moat, then serve.

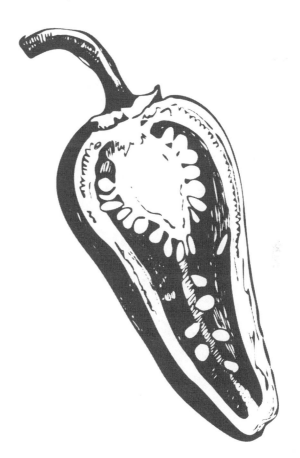

Tahini

Tahini originated in the Middle East, and is made from sesame seed kernels that have been toasted and ground to make a thick paste. Tahini is used in hummus, sauces, salad dressing, and other savory preparations, but can also be used like peanut butter as an ingredient in cookies!

Know Your Ingredients

Four More Ways to Make Hummus

1. Blend in 1 sun-dried tomato in oil for sun-dried tomato hummus.
2. Blend in the flesh of half a ripe avocado for avocado hummus (serve immediately, as avocado will discolor over time).
3. Blend in a few dashes of hot sauce for spicier hummus.
4. Top your hummus with chopped roasted nuts instead of salsa.

TECHNIQUE TAKEAWAY

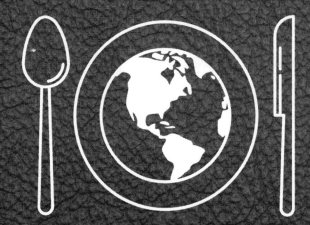

Four More Ways to Make Cheese Spread

1. Try swapping in pepper jack cheese for cheddar, or adding chopped fresh chives instead of sweet peppers.

2. You can also choose a different soft cheese, like Boursin, instead of plain cream cheese; or pick one of the many flavored cream cheeses that are available.

3. Add nuts for crunch, or tiny pieces of bacon or ham for a more savory touch.

4. Add a dash of hot sauce for heat or a spoonful of chopped sweet pickles for sweetness.

Pimento Cheese

The mild red peppers known as pimento peppers were originally called pimiento peppers and were imported from Spain as far back as the late 1800s. Around the turn of the 20th century, Americans integrated these sweet peppers into a mixture of cheese and mayonnaise, and pimento cheese spread was born.

Prep Time: 5 minutes
Cook Time: 0 minutes
Total Time: 5 minutes
Yield: 1 ½ cups

1. If you have a food processor, cut the cheddar into 4 to 6 chunks, place the chunks in the food processor with a standard chopping blade fitted, and pulse a few times until the cheddar is chopped into small pieces. If you don't have a food processor, use a cheese grater to grate the cheddar.
2. Mix the chopped or grated cheddar with all the other ingredients in a large mixing bowl until thoroughly combined. Serve immediately, or cover and refrigerate.

8 ounces extra sharp cheddar
3 ounces cream cheese, softened
½ cup drained and chopped
    pimento peppers
3 tablespoons mayonnaise
Pinch of ground black pepper (optional)

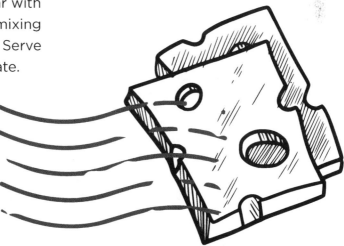

Herbes de Provence

Herbes de Provence is a mixture of dried rosemary, thyme, oregano, marjoram, and savory that is used in the cuisine of Provence, France. In the United States, dried lavender is also added to the dried herb mixture (most likely because of the association between Provence and lavender). Herbes de Provence is typically used to flavor meat, poultry, and seafood before or during the cooking process.

Know Your Ingredients

Herbes de Provence Dip

Americans love ranch dip, but did you know that a blend of French herbs makes a fantastic variation on the classic ranch flavor? All the ingredients for this dip (except the sour cream) can be kept on hand in the pantry for when the mood strikes. Herbes de Provence dip is equally suitable for dipping gluten free snacks like chips, pretzels, and crackers as it is for fresh veggies like broccoli and baby carrots.

Prep Time: 5 minutes
Cook Time: 0 minutes
Total Time: 5 minutes
Yield: 1 cup

For the Herbes de Provence blend:

1. Mix the herbs together to make the Herbes de Provence blend.

For the dip:

1. Combine all the dip ingredients and stir until well blended. Serve immediately, or cover tightly and refrigerate for 1 hour or more to allow the flavors to develop. Store leftover Herbes de Provence blend in the pantry in an airtight container; store leftover dip covered in the refrigerator.

For the Herbes de Provence blend:

2 teaspoons rosemary

2 teaspoons oregano

2 teaspoons savory

½ teaspoon marjoram

½ teaspoon thyme

¼ teaspoon lavender (optional)

For the dip:

1 tablespoon Herbes de Provence blend

⅛ teaspoon garlic powder

Pinch of onion powder

1 cup sour cream

Chipotle Dip

If you like smoky, spicy chipotle peppers, you're going to love this sour cream dip. Canned chipotle peppers in adobo sauce are one of the most versatile and flavorful ingredients you'll ever encounter. The quantity of peppers in your dip depends on your heat tolerance; add more peppers to spice it up, or cool it down by mixing in more sour cream.

Prep Time: 5 minutes
Cook Time: 0 minutes
Total Time: 5 minutes
Yield: 1 cup

1 to 3 canned chipotle peppers in adobo sauce (look for these in the Hispanic section of your grocery store)
1 cup sour cream, plus more if needed
1 tablespoon finely chopped fresh cilantro (optional)

1. Start with one chipotle pepper in adobo sauce; you can add more later if needed. Depending on how soft the pepper is, you can chop or smash it into a paste. There will be bits of pepper and seeds in the paste; that's expected.

2. Stir the chipotle pepper paste and cilantro (if used) into the sour cream. Taste the dip. If you want more spiciness, turn another pepper into paste and stir it in, too. Adjust as needed by adding another pepper to make it spicier, or adding more sour cream a tablespoon or two at a time to cool down the spiciness. Stir in the cilantro (optional).

Caprese Salad with Balsamic Reduction

Traditional *insalata caprese*, or Caprese salad, originated on the Italian island of Capri. This version adds a piquant balsamic vinegar syrup as a garnish.

Prep Time: 5 minutes
Cook Time: 5 minutes
Total Time: 10 minutes

1. Place the balsamic vinegar in a small saucepan and bring to a boil. The vinegar smell can become strong, so turn on a kitchen fan if you have one, and be careful not to overheat and burn the reduction. Reduce heat to low and let simmer, stirring occasionally, for about 5 to 10 minutes or until the sauce is slightly thickened and able to coat a spoon (the consistency of real maple syrup). While it cooks, prepare the salad itself, still keeping an eye on the progress of the balsamic reduction.

2. Cut the mozzarella into rounds. Rinse the basil and pat dry. Slice the tomatoes. When the reduction has thickened slightly, remove it from the heat and let cool.

3. Arrange the slices of tomatoes and mozzarella as desired (they can be served in individual stacks on salad plates, or as one large salad in family-style serving dish), then drizzle with olive oil and balsamic vinegar reduction. Garnish with freshly torn basil and serve immediately.

¾ cup of balsamic vinegar
8 ounces of fresh buffalo mozzarella
3 ripe flavorful tomatoes
Extra virgin olive oil, to garnish
1 ounce of fresh basil

Herb and Citrus Marinated Olives

Marinated olives are a traditional Greek accompaniment served as part of a meal or as a snack. They're packed with antioxidants and good fats. Try them paired with fresh bread, nuts, or a selection of meats and cheeses.

Prep Time: 20 minutes
Inactive Time: 24 hours
Yield: 3 ½ cups

2 teaspoons fennel seeds
3 cups pitted mixed Greek olives, rinsed and drained
2 tablespoons finely chopped mixed fresh herbs, such as rosemary, thyme, parsley, mint, etc.
2 teaspoons grated orange zest
2 teaspoons grated lemon zest
2 teaspoons grated lime zest
1 shallot finely chopped
2 garlic cloves minced
½ cup dry white wine
¼ cup extra virgin olive oil
2 tablespoons orange juice
2 tablespoons lemon juice
2 tablespoons lime juice
Pinch of ground cinnamon
Pinch of ground cumin

1. Toast the fennel seeds in a dry small skillet over medium heat, shaking the skillet frequently, until the seeds begin to pop and give off their aroma. Remove from the heat and transfer seeds to a plate to cool to room temperature.
2. Place the olives, fennel seeds, herbs, zests, shallot, and garlic in a bowl.
3. In a separate bowl, whisk together wine, oil, juices, cinnamon, and cumin. Pour over the olives.
4. Toss well then cover and place in refrigerator to marinate 1 to 2 days before serving. Stir or toss olives occasionally while marinating.

TECHNIQUE TAKEAWAY

How to Zest Citrus

Zesting citrus is easy with the right tool. Most large graters are too coarse for the delicate task of removing just the colorful peel while leaving bitter white pith intact. Pick up an inexpensive citrus zester, which will allow you to liberate the flavorful peel quickly and with no fuss.

Once you've mastered the technique, you can utilize citrus zest to perk up all kinds of salad dressings, marinades, and even cake frostings or glazes. If you don't have a citrus zester, you can lightly grate the peel against the smaller holes of a cheese grater; if the zest doesn't come out fine enough, you can chop it until it reaches an acceptable size.

French Green Lentil Salad

French green lentils are smaller, sturdier, and have a nuttier flavor than regular green or brown lentils. They're ideal for use in salads and soups where they need to hold their shape without turning to mush.

Prep Time: 10 minutes
Cook Time: 30 minutes
Total Time: 40 minutes
Yield: 3 cups

For the lentils:
1 pound French green lentils
   (about 2 ½ cups)
1 small onion, sliced in thick slices
1 large garlic clove, peeled and sliced in half
1 bay leaf
1 teaspoon kosher salt
¼ pound salt pork
½ teaspoon fresh ground black pepper

For the dressing:
½ cup red wine vinegar
¼ cup olive oil
2 teaspoons Dijon mustard
1 teaspoon kosher salt
½ teaspoon fresh ground black pepper
¼ cup finely chopped fresh parsley
1 teaspoon finely chopped fresh thyme leaves
1 teaspoon finely chopped rosemary
1 tablespoon finely chopped fresh basil

For the salad:
6 slices thick-sliced bacon, cooked and chopped

26

For the lentils:

1. Pick over the lentils, rinse and drain. In a large 6 quart pot, place the lentils, onion, garlic, bay leaf, salt, and pork. Add water and cover the ingredients by 2 to 3 inches. Bring to a boil over high heat. Reduce heat to low, cover, and simmer until the lentils are tender (about 20 to 25 minutes). Do not overcook lentils or they will be mushy. Drain lentils and discard the onion, garlic, bay leaf, and salt pork. Stir in pepper.

For the dressing:

1. In a large bowl, whisk together the vinegar, olive oil, mustard, salt, pepper, parsley, thyme, rosemary, and basil.

For the salad:

1. Add the lentils and bacon to the dressing. Stir to combine. Serve warm or at room temperature.

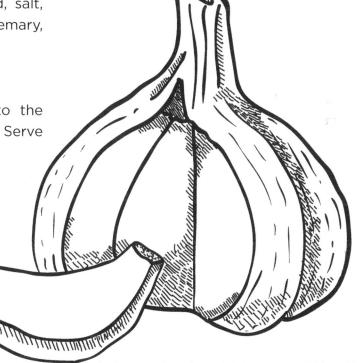

Greek Salad with Fresh Herb Vinaigrette

Greek salad is even better with a dressing made fresh from scratch. This version incorporates an abundance of green herbs into a base of good olive oil. Use high quality extra virgin olive oil for the best flavor.

Prep Time: 10 minutes
Cook Time: 0 minutes
Total Time: 10 minutes
Yield: 1 cup vinaigrette;
    salad quantity will vary

For the fresh herb vinaigrette:
1 teaspoon Dijon mustard
1 teaspoon honey
⅓ cup red wine vinegar
Pinch of salt or sea salt
Pinch of fresh ground pepper
½ clove garlic, chopped
½ small shallot, chopped
A few sprigs of fresh parsley
4 fresh basil leaves
1 teaspoon fresh thyme leaves
6 to 8 fresh rosemary leaves
½ to ⅔ cup extra virgin olive oil

For the Greek salad:
Fresh Herb Vinaigrette
Chopped romaine lettuce
Greek or Kalamata olives, pitted and cut in half lengthwise
Tomatoes cut into chunks or grape tomatoes cut in half lengthwise
Sweet 'n' Hot Salad Peppers (suggested brand: Mt. Olive)
Feta cheese
Pepperoncini

Optional or substitue toppings:
Cucumbers, peeled and chopped into small chunks
Red onion, thinly sliced
Bell pepper, thinly sliced
Shallot, thinly sliced
Banana pepper rings

Note: Ingredient amounts for the salad will vary depending on how many servings you'd like to make. and how large each portion will be.

For the fresh herb vinaigrette:

1. Put the mustard, honey, vinegar, salt, pepper, garlic, shallot, parsley, basil, thyme, and rosemary in a blender. Put the lid on and blend on high speed until ingredients are combined.

2. Turn the blender to low speed, remove the lid (or the middle of the lid), and slowly pour ½ cup of the olive oil in to the mixture. Turn blender off. Taste. If it has too much of a vinegar flavor, add more oil with the blender on low speed. Add in increments, stopping to taste, until it has the right oil/vinegar balance to you.

3. Pour into salad dressing shaker/container. Use immediately. Store leftover in refrigerator. Remember to take it out of the refrigerator about an hour before using again to get to room temperature. Shake to combine (it will separate).

For the Greek salad:

1. Put chopped romaine lettuce in a large bowl. Add some of the fresh herb vinaigrette to the lettuce (don't drown it; you can always add more to the finished salad as needed) and toss to coat.

1. Put the lettuce on a plate or plates. Top with olives, tomatoes, salad peppers, feta cheese, or any of the additional toppings. Place a few pepperoncini on the plate(s). Serve immediately.

Buttermilk Cornbread

Modern American cornbread was originally inspired by Native American recipes. Many variations of cornbread exist, from savory versions cooked in cast iron skillets to sweet versions that can be made into muffins. This cornbread recipe includes buttermilk, a classic ingredient in the cuisine of the southern United States, to provide a tangy balance to the sweetness.

Prep Time: 5 minutes
Cook Time: 15 minutes
Total Time: 20 minutes
Yield: 9 squares of cornbread

½ cup unsalted butter, plus a little more for greasing the pan
1 cup gluten free flour blend
1 cup gluten free cornmeal
¼ cup granulated sugar
½ teaspoon sea salt
1 ½ teaspoons baking powder
½ teaspoon baking soda
1 cup buttermilk
2 large eggs

1. Preheat the oven to 425°F. Lightly butter an 8 inch square pan and set aside. Melt the ½ cup of unsalted butter (do not overheat), and set aside to cool slightly.
2. In a large mixing bowl, combine the flour, cornmeal, sugar, salt, baking powder, and baking soda. Whisk thoroughly to combine. Make a well in the center of the dry ingredients.
3. In another bowl, lightly beat the eggs with the buttermilk. Pour the egg/buttermilk mixture into the well in the dry ingredients, then drizzle the melted butter in as well.
4. Gently fold the mixture together until everything is moist, but do not over mix. Scrape the batter evenly into the prepared pan and very lightly smooth the top (it will still be a little uneven, but will smooth out completely when baked).
5. Bake for about 15 to 20 minutes, or until a toothpick inserted in the middle comes out clean. Serve slightly warm.

TECHNIQUE TAKEAWAY

How to Make Your Own Buttermilk

No buttermilk? Make your own! Add 1 tablespoon of white vinegar to a measuring cup that holds 1 cup. Fill the rest of the measuring cup with milk. Stir together and let sit for 5 minutes, and you'll have a very close substitute for store-bought buttermilk.

Naan

Naan is Persian for "bread," and this type of puffy buttered flatbread can be found throughout central Asia and in India. This recipe produces smaller pieces of naan, which makes them easier to handle and faster to cook. Measuring the flour by weight ensures the precise ratio of flour to milk. It's essential to preheat the skillet before you make the dough; the goal is to get the naan into the hot pan as quickly as possible for the best result.

Prep Time: 5 minutes
Cook Time: 15 minutes
Total Time: 20 minutes
Yield: 16 small naan

Special equipment:
Large nonstick skillet

---

272 grams gluten free flour blend, plus extra for patting out the dough (recommended brand: Cup4Cup Multipurpose Flour)
1 ½ teaspoons baking powder
¾ teaspoon salt
2 teaspoons olive oil
1 cup warm milk
¼ cup salted butter, melted

1. Begin preheating a large nonstick skillet over medium heat.
2. Combine the flour, baking powder, and salt in a large mixing bowl. Whisk to combine. Drizzle the olive oil over the mixture and whisk again. Add the warm milk about ¼ cup at a time, mixing with a fork after each addition, until a soft and slightly sticky dough is formed.
3. Prepare a work surface by sprinkling lightly with flour. Dry and flour your hands. Scoop up a hunk of dough about the size of a golf ball and place it on the floured work surface. Pat it down a few times with the flats of your fingers, then flip it over and pat it down again into a circle or teardrop shape (teardrop is traditional), as thin as you can without tearing the dough or making it too difficult to peel off the work surface. It should be about 4½ inches in diameter.

4. Brush one side of the piece of naan with melted butter. Carefully peel the naan off the work surface and lay it butter side down in the hot skillet. Cook for about 30 to 60 seconds, or until the cooked side has brown dots all over, then quickly brush the uncooked side with butter and flip the piece of naan over to cook the other side for 30 to 60 seconds. When a piece of naan is done, remove it from the pan and cover to keep warm; you can add naan to this stack as you go.

5. Continue to form pieces of naan from the dough while watching the skillet. A large nonstick skillet will hold 3 or 4 pieces of naan at a time; rotate out the cooked pieces to make room for the uncooked pieces. Remember to brush one side with butter before placing it butter side down in the pan, and brush the uncooked side with butter before you flip it over to finish cooking.

6. If you have extra naan left over, they can be covered airtight and stored in the refrigerator, then reheated in a hot nonstick skillet. They can also be used as "flour" tortillas or for flatbread sandwiches.

Main Dishes

HANDHELD

Cuban Sandwich Sliders

By using gluten free rolls to make Cuban sandwich sliders, you get all the flavor of ham, pork, Swiss cheese, pickles, and mustard—and none of the gluten. Plus, you can prepare the sliders ahead of time. Prepare the sliders for baking and place the packets in the refrigerator until you're ready. Then proceed to the baking instructions.

Prep Time: 5 minutes
Cook Time: 13 minutes
Total Time: 18 minutes
Yield: 8 sliders, or 4 servings

---

8 small gluten free rolls
¼ pound sliced Swiss cheese
½ pound thin sliced sweet ham
½ pound sliced roast pork
Yellow mustard
Dill pickle slices
3 tablespoons unsalted butter, softened

1. Preheat the oven to 400°F. Lay out four sheets of foil; each should be larger than one group of 4 rolls (big enough enough to crimp the edges together later).
2. Using a serrated knife, horizontally cut through each roll, creating a top and a bottom. Open up all the rolls and spread mustard all over the inside of the top and the inside of the bottom. On each bottom, layer sweet ham, then sliced pork, then slices of swiss cheese, and finally a layer of sliced dill pickles. Replace the top halves of the rolls.
3. Gently rub the softened butter all over the tops, bottoms, and sides of the rolls. Once the sliders are thoroughly coated, place 4 rolls in the center of one sheet of foil and 4 rolls in the center of a second sheet of foil. Place the remaining foil sheets on top of each group of 4 rolls. Pinch or roll the edges of the top and bottom foil tightly to seal the sliders inside like a packet.
4. Place both foil packets on a baking sheet. Bake for 8 minutes, then carefully flip both packets over and bake for 5 more minutes. Remove from oven and let cool for 2 minutes before opening the packets to serve.

Four More Ways to Make Oven Baked Sliders

1. Layer pepperoni and mozzarella for pizza sliders.
2. Stack roast beef and Swiss cheese with a little horseradish sauce brushed on the inside of the rolls.
3. Pile shredded leftover chicken mixed with BBQ sauce on the rolls and top with pepper jack cheese for southwestern BBQ sliders.
4. Spread the inside of rolls with Thousand Island or Russian dressing, then pile on corned beef, sauerkraut, and Swiss cheese for mini Reuben sliders.

Grilled Pork Lettuce Cups

Enlivened with Asian flavors such as fresh ginger and cilantro, these pork lettuce cups contain everything you need for a complete meal: protein, vegetables, and even a bit of fruit.

Prep Time: 30 minutes
Inactive Time: 3 hours
Cook Time: 30 minutes
Total Time: 4 hours
Yield: 4 servings

¾ cup fresh cilantro, divided
Grated zest of 1 lime
¼ cup lime juice
2 tablespoons sweet white wine
1 tablespoon honey
1 tablespoon grated fresh ginger
1 garlic clove, minced
1 green onion, thinly sliced
3 tablespoons canola oil, divided,
    plus more for brushing
1 pork tenderloin,
    approximately 1 pound
1 peach
1 package coleslaw mix,
    approximately 14 ounces
4 radishes, very thinly sliced
1 jalapeño pepper, very thinly sliced
1 head Boston lettuce, separated

1. Finely chop ¼ cup cilantro and place in a small bowl. Add lime zest, juice, wine, honey, ginger, garlic, green onion, and 1 tablespoon oil. Whisk to combine.
2. Transfer ¼ cup dressing to a large plastic zip top bag. Cover remaining dressing and chill.
3. Trim off and discard any fat or silver skin from the pork. Tie the pork tenderloin for even cooking. Add pork to the bag and seal, pressing out as much air as possible.
4. Marinate pork in the refrigerator at least 2 hours or overnight.
5. Remove pork from the refrigerator and allow it to get to room temperature, about 1 to 1 ½ hours.
6. Heat grill to medium-high. Remove pork from the marinade and grill, covered, until the internal temperature is 145°F, about 18 to 20 minutes. Turn pork a few times while grilling for even cooking. Discard marinade.
7. Transfer pork to a cutting board, loosely cover with foil, and let rest for 10 minutes before slicing.

8. Cut peach into 10 or 12 wedges. Discard the pit. Brush peach slices with oil. Grill slices until slightly charred, about 1 to 2 minutes per side. Cut peach slices into halves or thirds (to make them bite-sized).
9. Thinly slice pork and transfer to a serving plate.
10. Whisk 2 tablespoons oil into the dressing.
11. Combine coleslaw mix, radish slices, jalapeño slices, and remaining cilantro (chopped) in a large bowl. Pour dressing over slaw and toss to coat. Gently stir in peaches.
12. Serve slaw with sliced pork and lettuce leaves.

Quesadilla Cheese

An entire book could be written on the many types and uses of Mexican cheese. The cheese known as "quesadilla cheese" in the United States is asadero cheese, which melts smoothly without separating, making it perfect for stuffing quesadillas. Don't confuse authentic quesadilla cheese with the pre-shredded bags of Monterey Jack blends; they're quite different from one another.

Know Your Ingredients

Carne Asada Burgers

This recipe uses a simple Mexican marinade with a palate-pleasing balance of acidic lime juice, pungent garlic, and salt, brought together in a base of extra virgin olive oil.

Prep Time: 5 minutes
Cook Time: 10 minutes
Total Time: 15 minutes
Yield: 4 burgers

---

1. To make the marinade, blend the lime juice, garlic cloves, salt, pepper, oil, and water until mostly liquid. (If you don't have a blender, you can use a mortar and pestle to grind the garlic, salt, and pepper into a paste, then whisk it into the lime juice, oil and water.)
2. In a large mixing bowl, combine the ground beef with the carne asada marinade. Mix until thoroughly combined. Shape into 4 patties.
3. Preheat a nonstick skillet to medium high heat. Cook burgers for about 3 minutes on one side, followed by 6 minutes on the other side, or until the burgers reach the doneness you prefer. Place the cooked burgers on buns and garnish with your choice of toppings (add quesadilla cheese while the burger is hot, to allow it melt).

For the marinade:
3 teaspoons lime juice
2 garlic cloves
½ teaspoon sea salt
¼ teaspoon ground black pepper
1 teaspoon extra virgin olive oil
2 teaspoons water

For the burgers:
1 pound ground beef
4 gluten free hamburger buns

Toppings:
Quesadilla cheese, shredded
Salsa
Chopped jalapeños
Chopped tomatoes
Chopped cilantro

Meatball Subs

These comfort food sandwiches feature Italian-style meatballs piled on gluten free submarine rolls and covered in melted mozzarella cheese.

Prep Time: 10 minutes
Cook Time: 20 minutes
Total Time: 30 minutes
Yield: 12 meatballs

For the meatballs:

⅓ cup gluten free cracker crumbs
(recommended brand: Schar
Table Crackers)

2 teaspoons Italian seasoning

¼ teaspoon garlic powder

¼ teaspoon salt

⅓ cup grated Parmesan cheese

1 pound lean ground beef

24 ounces spaghetti sauce, divided

For the subs:

4 gluten free sub rolls

8 slices mozzarella cheese

For the meatballs:

1. Preheat oven to 400°F. Mix together the cracker crumbs, Italian seasoning, garlic powder, salt, and grated Parmesan cheese. Set aside.
2. In a large mixing bowl, combine the ground sirloin and ⅓ cup spaghetti sauce. Mix until the sauce is evenly distributed through the beef. Then, mix in the cracker crumb mixture until it is evenly distributed through the beef.
3. Form meatballs approximately 1 ½ to 2 inches in diameter. You should end up with about 12 meatballs. Place the meatballs evenly in a baking dish so that they are not touching. (You can line this baking dish with parchment paper to prevent sticking, if desired.)
4. Bake for 20 minutes at 400°F, or until the internal temperature of a meatball measured with an instant read thermometer equals 160°F or greater. Heat the remaining spaghetti sauce in a saucepan until steaming hot (do not boil), and add the baked meatballs to the sauce keep warm until the sub rolls are ready to fill.

For the subs:

1. Split open the sub rolls and toast them for 3 to 4 minutes in the oven. Add meatballs and a little sauce to each roll, then top each sub with two slices of mozzarella cheese. Return the subs to the oven for 3 to 4 minutes, or until the cheese melts. Serve immediately.

Buffalo Chicken Lettuce Wraps

Buffalo wings are an American invention that originated at the Anchor Bar in Buffalo, New York in 1964. The original Buffalo wings were deep fried, but this version swaps in leftover shredded chicken as a better-for-you recipe makeover that's served in lettuce cups.

Prep Time: 5 minutes
Cook Time: 0 minutes
Total Time: 5 minutes
Yield: 8 wraps

1. Stir the buffalo wing sauce into the shredded chicken until the chicken pieces are thoroughly coated. Lay out the lettuce leaves.
2. Spoon equal portions of the sauce-coated chicken on to each lettuce leaf. Drizzle with the dressing of your choice. Sprinkle on chopped celery and serve immediately.

½ cup Buffalo wing sauce
2 cups shredded chicken
8 leaves butter lettuce (or similar lettuce suitable for making lettuce cups)
½ cup blue cheese or ranch dressing
⅔ cup chopped celery

Chipotle Pinto Bean Tacos with Creamy Avocado Sauce

This taco recipe is ready to enjoy in just ten minutes, making it possibly the fastest taco recipe on record. A chipotle pepper in adobo sauce adds smoky, spicy complexity to the beans, while the creamy avocado sauce cools everything down.

Prep Time: 5 minutes
Cook Time: 5 minutes
Total Time: 10 minutes
Yield: 4 servings

For the chipotle sauce:
1 chipotle in adobo sauce
¼ cup tomato puree
2 tablespoons vegetable broth
1 teaspoon olive oil
1 teaspoon fresh oregano, minced
    (substitute with ½ teaspoon dried oregano
    if desired)
1 teaspoon cumin
½ teaspoon garlic powder
½ teaspoon salt
pinch of black pepper

For the creamy avocado sauce:
2 avocados, peeled and halved, pits removed
2 cloves garlic, chopped
1 cup plain vegan yogurt (or substitute plain
    Greek yogurt), equal to a
    5.3 ounce container
¼ cup packed cilantro, roughly chopped
½ teaspoon salt
Juice of 1 lime

To be added after the chipotle sauce is made:
(2) 16 ounce cans pinto beans,
    drained and rinsed

To serve:
Gluten free tortillas
Chopped lettuce
Chopped tomatoes
Chopped red onion

1. Add all the ingredients for chipotle sauce into a food processor. Pulse until smooth.
2. Heat a medium sized saucepan over low to medium heat. While your saucepan heats, transfer chipotle sauce to a small bowl. Rinse the food processor bowl (with its blade still in place) under warm water until clean. Add all avocado sauce ingredients into the food processor. Pulse until smooth and creamy.
3. When the pan is heated, add the chipotle sauce into the saucepan, then the beans. Stir until well combined and heat until warm, about 4 minutes. Turn off heat and remove from burner.
4. Fill your tortillas with beans and desired toppings, then top with creamy avocado sauce.

Recipe contributed by Scott Burgett, founder of PlantBasedScotty.com.

POST MAIL

POST MAIL

Tofu

Tofu is made from soybeans and comes in many varieties, such as silken, soft, medium, firm, and extra-firm. The more firm the tofu, the more water has been pressed out of it. Silken tofu can be used in smoothies and puddings, while the more firm varieties of tofu are better for stir-frying. Tofu is high in protein and is often used as a meat substitute for vegetarians, and it's also notable for its ability to soak up the flavor of whatever it's cooked with.

Nutritional Yeast

Nutritional yeast is a flavoring ingredient that's often used in vegan recipes to provide a cheesy or nutty flavor. It's a different strain from the type of yeast that's used to leaven bread. Use nutritional yeast like you would use Parmesan cheese, as a topping for vegetables, salads, popcorn, and other savory recipes.

Know Your Ingredients

Portobello Mushrooms and Tofu Scramble Ciabatta Sandwich

The introduction of ciabatta bread to Great Britain in the early 1980s helped Mediterranean-inspired cuisine become a staple of the British diet. This vegan ciabatta sandwich is packed with flavor and nutrition.

Prep Time: 5 minutes
Cook Time: 20 minutes
Total Time: 25 minutes
Yield: 2 servings

---

1. Preheat a skillet to medium heat.
2. Brush portobello mushrooms with olive oil. Cook in the skillet for 8 minutes on each side. Remove to a plate and cover to keep warm.
3. In the heated skillet, scramble the tofu with a fork. Add turmeric, thyme and nutritional yeast. While the tofu is heating up, cut ciabatta rolls in half horizontally and toast them. Stir the tofu mixture well and continue to heat until it's warm. Season with salt and pepper to taste.
4. Spread pesto inside each toasted ciabatta half. For each sandwich, sprinkle ciabatta bottom with alfalfa sprouts and red onions. Stack 1 mushroom on top, followed by ¼ of the tofu scramble and 1 piece of roasted pepper. Sprinkle with more alfalfa sprouts and cover with ciabatta top. Serve with Kalamata olives (optional).

4 whole portobello mushrooms
Olive oil
12 ounces firm tofu
½ teaspoon turmeric
½ teaspoon dried thyme
2 tablespoons nutritional yeast
Salt and pepper
¼ cup sun-dried tomato pesto
4 small ciabatta rolls (recommended brand: Schar Ciabatta Rolls)
2 roasted peppers, each cut in two pieces
Small bunch of alfalfa sprouts
¼ red onion, finely chopped
Kalamata olives (optional)

Recipe contributed by Caleb Backe, a personal trainer and expert in health and wellness for MapleHolistics.com.

POST MAIL
POST MAIL

Salsa Verde

Mexican salsa verde is a salsa made with tomatillos. Tomatillos are related to tomatoes, but are green when ripe and have a tart flavor. To make salsa verde, chopped tomatillos are typically mixed with onions, peppers, salt, and cilantro.

Know Your Ingredients

Salsa Verde Quesadillas

Quesadillas are an excellent way to use up leftover protein like steak, shrimp, chicken, or pork. Tossing your chosen protein with a little salsa verde adds fresh flavor that pairs well with melty quesadilla cheese.

Prep Time: 5 minutes
Cook Time: 10 minutes
Total Time: 15 minutes
Yield: 4 small quesadillas

1. Toss the protein with the salsa to coat.
2. Preheat a large nonstick pan on medium low heat for a few minutes.
3. When the pan is hot, place 4 corn tortillas in the pan (do not overlap).
4. Sprinkle ¼ cup shredded cheese and ½ cup protein on each tortilla, then add another tortilla on top. Cook the quesadilla for about 3 minutes, or until there are toasty brown spots on the outside of the bottom corn tortilla, then use a large turner to carefully flip the quesadilla over. Continue cooking until the cheese is melted and there are brown spots on the outside of the other tortilla.
5. Repeat with more tortillas, protein, and cheese.
6. Serve immediately.

4 cups cooked protein of choice,
 such as steak, shrimp, chicken, or pork,
 in bite sized chunks
½ cup salsa verde
16 small corn tortillas
2 cups shredded quesadilla cheese

Main Dishes

FORK & KNIFE

Beef Stifado

Stifado, sometimes spelled *stifatho*, is Greek for "stew." This aromatic, slow-cooked beef stew is flavored with tomatoes, wine, and spices. It's traditionally served with orzo (Greek pasta), but it's also fantastic when served with toasted gluten free bread to soak up the rich sauce.

Prep Time: 15 minutes
Cook Time: 3 hours
Total Time: 3 hours 15 minutes
Yield: 6 servings

1. Prepare the shallots for peeling by boiling for 3 minutes, then rinsing with cool water until they are cool enough to handle. Peel the shallots, but leave them whole.
2. Chop the garlic.
3. In a small cup, mix together the allspice, nutmeg, and oregano. Set the spice mix aside.
4. Preheat a Dutch oven on the stove on medium heat. Add the olive oil. When the pot is hot, brown the roast on all sides, then set aside on a plate.
5. Toss the shallots, the garlic, and the spice mix in the pot. Saute for 30 seconds until fragrant. Add the crushed tomatoes, tomato paste, and red wine. Stir to combine, then drop in the bay leaves.
6. Place the roast back in the pot. Drop in the potatoes. Add a little water so that the level of the liquid is just barely covering the meat and potatoes.
7. Cover tightly with a lid and simmer for one hour. Remove the lid and continue simmering for 1 ½ to 2 hours, or until the roast can be easily cut with a spoon. (If the level of liquid goes too low, add a bit of water. This is pretty unlikely, though.)
8. When the beef stifado is done, if there are small puddles of oil on top of the liquid, you may spoon them out if you like.

3 ounces shallots, about 2 or 3 large shallots
3 cloves garlic
½ teaspoon allspice
1 pinch nutmeg
1 teaspoon dried oregano
1 ½ pounds boneless chuck roast (up to 1 ¾ pounds)
2 tablespoons olive oil
28 ounces canned crushed tomatoes
1 tablespoon tomato paste
1 cup red wine
1 tablespoon red wine vinegar
1 pound petite red potatoes
Gluten free bread, toasted, for serving (optional)

Tamari Soy Sauce

Traditional soy sauce is brewed with wheat. Tamari soy sauce, on the other hand, is soy sauce made with little or no wheat. That means it's still important to check the label to make sure the soy sauce is gluten free. Traditional soy sauce and tamari soy sauce have a similar flavor, although tamari soy sauce is slightly thicker and darker.

Red Curry Paste

Curry pastes are a staple of Thai cuisine. They come in several varieties, including green curry paste, yellow curry paste, and red curry paste. Curry pastes contain different combinations of ingredients with varying levels of heat, and are usually mixed with coconut milk and other liquids to make a rich sauce that can be used on meats and vegetables. You can find curry paste in the spice aisle or the Asian food section of your grocery store.

Know Your Ingredients

Red Curry Shrimp Zoodles

"Zoodles," vegetable-based noodles made from spiralized zucchini and yellow squash, take the place of the rice that traditionally accompanies Thai red curry. It's an easy way to add more vegetables while still enjoying all the rich flavor of the curry. If you don't have a spiralizer, you can use a vegetable peeler to slice thin pieces of zucchini and yellow squash.

Prep Time: 10 minutes
Inactive Time: 1 hour
Cook Time: 20 minutes
Total Time: 1 hour 30 minutes
Yield: 4 servings

1. Lay paper towels on a work surface (4 layers of 2 sheets wide). Sprinkle about ½ teaspoon salt on the towels.
2. Spread spiralized squashes evenly on the paper towels. Sprinkle about ½ teaspoon salt on the squash.
3. Lay paper towels on top of squash (4 layers of 2 sheets wide) and press down.
4. Allow salt to pull moisture from the squashes for about an hour. Press down on paper towels occasionally.
5. Whisk together coconut milk, tamari, tahini, curry paste, vinegar, honey, ginger, lime juice, and garlic in a large skillet or saute pan. Bring to boil then reduce heat to simmer, whisking occasionally. Simmer for 10 minutes.
6. Add shrimp and cook until shrimp begins to turn opaque, about 2 to 3 minutes. Add squash and toss to coat with sauce.
7. Cook until shrimp are done and squash has slightly softened, about 5 minutes.
8. Transfer to a serving platter or bowls. Garnish with cilantro. Serve with lime wedges.

2 zucchini squash, spiralized
1 yellow squash, spiralized
½ cup coconut milk
⅓ cup low-sodium gluten free tamari soy sauce
¼ cup well-stirred tahini
2 tablespoons red curry paste
1 tablespoon apple cider vinegar
1 tablespoon honey
1 tablespoon ginger paste or ground fresh ginger
Juice of 1 lime
1 garlic clove, minced or crushed
¾ pound raw shrimp
Chopped fresh cilantro for garnish
Lime wedges for serving

Grilled Chimichurri Skirt Steak

Although traditional Argentine chimichurri sauce is used as a topping, not a marinade, in this recipe chimichurri pulls double duty. By using it as a marinade before grilling, it adds delectable depth of flavor.

Prep Time: 15 minutes
Inactive Time: 1 hour
Cook Time: 15 minutes
Total Time: 1 hour 30 minutes
Yield: 4 to 6 servings,
   depending on the weight of
   the steak and the serving size

For the chimichurri sauce:
1 bunch fresh flat-leaf parsley
1 bunch fresh cilantro
¼ cup packed fresh oregano leaves
3 teaspoons fresh thyme leaves
1 ½ teaspoon chopped fresh rosemary leaves
1 serrano pepper, seeded and chopped
3 tablespoons red wine vinegar
½ teaspoon red pepper flakes
½ teaspoon salt
¼ teaspoon fresh ground pepper
½ cup olive oil, plus more if needed

For the steak:
1 to 2 pound skirt steak
Salt and pepper

For the chimichrri:

1. Make sure all the fresh herbs have been rinsed and dried. Cut the stems from the parsley and cilantro below the leaves (to have mostly only leaves left).
2. Place the parsley, cilantro, oregano, thyme, rosemary, serrano pepper, vinegar, red pepper flakes, salt, and pepper in the bowl of a food processor fitted with a knife blade.
3. Pulse a few times to chop the herbs. Scrape down the sides of the bowl. Pulse while drizzling in the olive oil. Do not over-process or it will become a paste.
4. Transfer the chimichurri sauce to a small bowl. Stir in additional olive oil for desired consistency. Adjust seasoning with salt and pepper to taste.
5. Use immediately or cover and refrigerate overnight. If desired, it can be made ahead to allow the flavors to develop.

For the steak:

1. Spread about ⅓ to ½ of the chimichurri sauce on both sides of the steak. Let marinate for 1 hour on the counter while the steak is coming to room temperature.
2. Heat a grill to medium-high heat (about 450 to 500°F)
3. Cut steak in half crosswise with the grain. Scrape off most of the chimichurri and discard (to prevent the taste of burnt herbs).
4. Sprinkle salt and pepper on both sides of the steak.
5. Grill the steaks until medium-rare (or your preferred doneness), about 2 to 4 minutes per side, depending on thickness of steak.
6. Remove steak from the grill and cover loosely with foil. Let rest for 10 minutes.
7. Thinly slice steak at an angle across the grain.
8. Arrange steak slices on a platter with some of the chimichurri sauce on top.
9. Serve immediately with remaining chimichurri on the side

TECHNIQUE TAKEAWAY

Five More Ways to Use Chimichurri Sauce

1. Try topping chicken, shrimp, or fish with chimichurri sauce.
2. Use it as a substitute for (or in addition to) salsa for tacos.
3. Add it to your baked potato toppings.
4. Stir it into sour cream to make a chimichurri flavored dip.
5. Spread it on toasted gluten free bread to make a fresh and flavorful alternative to garlic bread.

Beef Stroganoff

Beef Stroganoff is a dish of Russian origin, created by a chef who named It after his employer, Count Pavel Aleksandrovich Stroganoff. This variation is lightened up by using Greek yogurt instead of sour cream.

Prep Time: 10 minutes
Cook Time: 25 minutes
Total Time: 35 minutes
Yield: 4 servings

1. Bring a large pot of salted water to a boil. Cook the egg noodles according to package directions. Drain and reserve.
2. Heat a large saute pan over medium-high heat. Toss the beef with salt and pepper to taste. Heat the oil and saute beef just long enough to get some browning, about 1 minute per side. Remove to a plate.
3. Add the onion and mushroom to the pan. Cook until lightly browned, about 5 minutes. Deglaze the pan with the cognac. Add the beef stock and Dijon mustard. Cook until reduced by about one quarter. Remove the pan from the heat, and stir in the yogurt, dill and reserved beef.
4. Divide noodles between 4 bowls. Top with meat and sauce, then sprinkle with paprika.

4 ounces gluten free egg noodles
2 tablespoons vegetable oil
12 ounces beef tenderloin, sliced into strips approximately ¼ inch wide
    by 2 inches long
1 cup thinly sliced onion
1 ½ cups button mushrooms,
    thinly sliced
¼ cup cognac
1 cup no sodium added beef stock
1 tablespoon Dijon mustard
¾ cup plain Greek yogurt
2 tablespoons finely chopped fresh dill
1 teaspoon paprika.

Recipe contributed by the National Pasta Association (NPA).

Three Cheese Pastitsio

Pastitsio is a Greek main dish made from pasta, cinnamon-spiced ground beef in tomato sauce, and creamy cheese sauce. This version uses three types of cheese—Parmesan, Romano, and white cheddar—to make it extra cheesy.

Prep Time: 5 minutes
Cook Time: 45 minutes to make the pasta, beef, and cheese sauce; 45 minutes to bake
Total Time: 1 hour 35 minutes
Yield: 6 servings

For the pasta:
8 ounces gluten free macaroni (or substitute penne)

For the ground beef in tomato sauce:
1 pound ground beef (ground round or lean ground beef, whichever you prefer)
1 garlic clove, finely chopped, or 1/8 teaspoon garlic powder
1 cup beef stock
½ cup tomato sauce
1 tablespoon tomato paste
1 teaspoon ground cinnamon
½ teaspoon ground cumin

For the cheese sauce:
¼ cup salted butter
⅓ cup gluten free flour blend (recommended brand: Cup4Cup Multipurpose Flour)
½ cup milk
½ cup plain Greek yogurt
½ cup grated Romano cheese
½ cup grated Parmesan cheese

For assembly:
2 cups shredded extra sharp white cheddar

For the pasta:
1. Boil and drain the gluten free pasta according to the package directions. Set aside. Begin preheating the oven to 350°F.

For the ground beef in tomato sauce:
1. In a large frying pan over medium heat, cook the beef and garlic together, breaking the beef into crumbles as it cooks, for about 10 minutes. When the beef is fully cooked, add the beef stock, tomato sauce, tomato paste, cinnamon, and cumin to the pan. Stir together, reduce heat, and simmer for 15 minutes while you make the cheese sauce.

For the cheese sauce:
1. In a saucepan over medium heat, melt the butter. Whisk in the flour and continue to cook for about 1 minute until smooth. Remove the saucepan from the heat. Whisk in the milk and Greek yogurt a little at a time until smooth; it may look curdled at first, but it will smooth out. Return to heat. Add a pinch of ground nutmeg, then incorporate the Parmesan and Romano cheese about ¼ cup at a time, whisking after each addition, until the cheese sauce is smooth and hot. It will be thick.

For assembly:
1. Stir the cheese sauce into the cooked pasta until evenly distributed. Scoop half of the pasta into a 2 quart casserole dish and smooth it into an even layer. Pour the meat sauce over the bottom layer of pasta. Scoop the remaining pasta over the layer of meat sauce and smooth it into an even layer. Sprinkle the shredded white cheddar evenly over the top of the pasta, all the way to the edges.
2. Bake for about 45 minutes, or until lightly browned on top. Let cool slightly before serving.

Moroccan Rice

Ras el hanout is a Moroccan spice mixture; it translates from Arabic as "head of the shop," which is like saying something is "top shelf" or of the best quality. Many grocery stores carry this spice mix pre-made, but in case your grocery store doesn't stock it, you'll find instructions to make your own accompanying this recipe. Feel free to use up leftovers by swapping in your favorite protein, adding some cooked veggies, or using a different gluten free grain, such as cooked quinoa.

Prep Time: 5 minutes
Cook Time: 0 minutes
Total Time: 5 minutes
Yield: 4 servings

---

4 cups warm cooked rice
2 cups warm chopped
    cooked chicken
4 teaspoons ras el hanout spice mix
¼ cup sliced almonds or
    slivered almonds
¼ cup golden raisins

1. Combine all ingredients and mix well.

How to Make Your Own Ras El Hanout

Mix the spices and salt together, then use a teaspoon or so of the resulting mixture to flavor meats, marinades, or even popcorn!

1 teaspoon ground cumin
1 teaspoon ground ginger
1 teaspoon salt
¾ teaspoon ground black pepper
½ teaspoon ground cinnamon
½ teaspoon cayenne
½ teaspoon ground allspice
¼ teaspoon ground cloves

Kässpätzle

Kässpätzle is German for cheese spätzle. The word *spätzle* itself means "little sparrows," referring to the shape of the hand-formed noodles. This rich dish comes from the Swabian area of Germany, which is known for its hearty, down-to-earth cuisine. Ingredient quantities are given in weight for precision measurement, which makes it easier to get the recipe right.

Prep Time: 20 minutes
Cook Time: 10 minutes
Total Time: 30 minutes
Yield: 4 servings

---

3 medium sized eggs
300 to 400 milliliters milk
50 grams gluten free flour blend
50 grams potato starch
1 heaped teaspoon salt
1 to 2 spring onions
2 tablespoons butter
350 grams grated Gouda cheese

1. Beat eggs and add a portion of the milk. Add flour, starch and salt and make a smooth dough. Add only as much of the remaining milk as needed.
2. Let dough rest for 10 minutes.
3. In the meantime, put plenty of salted water on to boil. Peel and slice the spring onions, then fry them with butter in a pan.
4. Scrape the spätzle dough through a spätzle slicer or directly from a cutting board into the boiling water in batches, and scoop them out when they come to surface.
5. After they're removed from the water, layer the spätzle with grated cheese in a casserole dish. Place the casserole in a warm oven between batches until all of the dough is used up.
6. Add the spring onions and serve.

Recipe contributed by Kati Schmidt, co-founder of glutenfreiheit.org.

POST MAIL
POST MAIL

Potato Starch

Potato starch is a versatile ingredient that's frequently used in gluten free recipes. It's made by crushing potatoes, then washing out and drying the released starch. Potato starch can function as a thickener, like cornstarch, or improve texture by adding fluffiness.

Know Your Ingredients

Italian Frittata

Frittatas can be served hot or cold, for breakfast, brunch, lunch or dinner, made with almost any kind of savory meat and vegetable fillings that you can imagine. This frittata includes Italian sausage, mozzarella cheese, mushrooms, and grape

Prep Time: 10 minutes
Cook Time: 30 minutes
Total Time: 40 minutes
Yield: 4 servings

---

8 eggs
¼ cup heavy cream, half-and-half, or milk
Salt and pepper
1 cup shredded mozzarella cheese, divided
4 ounces Italian sausage
8 ounces sliced baby portobello mushrooms
1 cup grape tomatoes, sliced in half

1. Preheat the oven to 375°F. In a medium bowl, whisk together the eggs and cream. Season the mixture with salt and pepper, add ½ cup shredded cheese, and stir to combine.
2. Heat a large ovenproof skillet over medium-high heat. Cook the Italian sausage into crumbles until browned. Add the mushrooms and cook until tender. Add the tomatoes to the skillet and cook for 1 minute.
3. Distribute all the fillings evenly around the pan, then pour the egg mixture over everything. Sprinkle the remaining ½ cup shredded cheese over the top. Cook on the stovetop for 2 minutes, and then transfer pan to the oven. Bake for 20 minutes or until the eggs have set.
4. Cool in the pan for 10 minutes then transfer frittata to a serving platter. Slice and enjoy. Leftovers can be refrigerated and served cold or reheated.

TECHNIQUE TAKEAWAY

Five More Ingredient Combinations to Use in a Frittata

1. Cooked broccoli + cheddar cheese
2. Cooked spinach + gruyère cheese
3. Chopped ham + Swiss cheese + chopped cooked asparagus
4. Cooked crumbled bacon + blue cheese crumbles + halved grape tomatoes
5. Chopped roasted red peppers + quesadilla cheese + sliced avocado

Oat Flour Pancakes

Why not make pancakes for dinner? Inspired by the traditional ingredients used in Scottish oatcakes, these pancakes use oat flour instead of wheat flour to make fluffy American-style pancakes. Pancake batter is always best when used as soon as it's made; if you save it overnight, your pancakes may turn out flat because the leavener loses its bubbly power.

Prep Time: 5 minutes
Cook Time: 15 minutes
Total Time: 20 minutes
Yield: 12 pancakes

For the dry mix:
1 ½ cups gluten free oat flour (180 grams)
2 tablespoons granulated sugar
2 teaspoons baking powder
½ teaspoon salt

For the wet mix:
4 tablespoons salted butter, melted
1 cup buttermilk
1 teaspoon pure vanilla extract
2 large eggs
½ cup water

1. Preheat a nonstick skillet over medium low heat while you prepare the pancake batter.
2. In a large mixing bowl, whisk together the dry mix ingredients. In a second mixing bowl, whisk together the wet ingredients. Make a well in the center of the dry mix bowl.
3. Test the skillet by flicking a few drops of water into the center. If the pan is hot enough, they should immediately sizzle away.
4. Once the skillet is hot, pour the wet mix into the dry mix and whisk thoroughly. The batter should be pourable; if it's too thick, whisk in more water 1 tablespoon at a time until it is able to pour at a slow but even rate.
5. Add batter to the skillet, about ¼ cup per pancake (a large skillet can cook two pancakes at a time). Cook until air bubbles form and stay open, and the outer edges are mostly solidified. Turn, and cook until the center puffs up completely. Remove to a plate and cover to keep warm. Repeat with remaining batter.
6. If the pancakes begin to overbrown before they cook through, the skillet has gotten too hot. Turn the heat down slightly and continue.

POST MAIL

POST MAIL

Oat Flour

Oat flour is produced by grinding oats into a fine powder. Since oats are frequently farmed, transported, stored, or processed alongside grains that contain gluten, it's important to check your oat flour to make sure that it's gluten free. Some companies rely on mechanical sorting to remove contaminating grains, while others follow the strict "Purity Protocol" guidelines for producing gluten free oats. Some people are more sensitive to cross-contamination than others, so shop carefully according to your needs.

For this pancake recipe, you can also substitute other gluten free flours for the oat flour. Sorghum flour is an excellent substitute for oat flour in this pancake recipe, and so are many well-known gluten free flour blends. Measure flour by weight, not volume, for the best results.

Know Your Ingredients

Desserts

Rice Cream with Cherry Sauce

Scandinavian rice cream is a traditional Christmas dessert made from leftover rice porridge. It's creamy, fluffy, and shouldn't be confused with rice pudding, which is much denser. Rice cream with cherry sauce is especially beautiful when served in clear glasses that showcase the contrast between the white rice cream and the dark red cherry sauce.

Prep Time: 10 minutes
Cook Time: 40 minutes
Inactive Time: 1 hour
Total Time: 1 hour 50 minutes
Yield: 8 servings

For the cherry sauce:
¼ cup water
1 tablespoon lemon juice
1 tablespoon sugar
Pinch of salt
2 tablespoons cornstarch
2 cups frozen cherries

For the rice cream:
1 ½ cups water
¼ teaspoon salt
1 cup short-grain white rice
2 cups milk
¼ cup slivered almonds (optional)
1 cup heavy cream
¼ cup granulated sugar
1 teaspoon pure vanilla extract

For the cherry sauce:
1. Combine the water, lemon juice, sugar, salt, and cornstarch in a small pot. Whisk until completely smooth.
2. Add the frozen cherries and stir to coat. Bring the mixture to a boil over medium heat and cook for 5 minutes, stirring occasionally. Remove from heat and let cool. Cover and refrigerate to store until the rice cream is ready to serve.

For the rice cream:

1. Combine the water, salt, and rice in a pot. Bring to a boil, then reduce heat to low, cover, and simmer for 15 to 20 minutes, or until all the water has been absorbed and the rice is tender. Pour the milk into the pot, bring it to a boil again, and then reduce the heat to low, cover, and let it simmer for another 15 to 20 minutes, or until the milk has been absorbed.

2. When the rice has absorbed all the milk, remove it from the pot into a large mixing bowl, stir in the almonds (if used), then let the mixture cool for about 1 hour or until it reaches room temperature, stirring occasionally to aid the cooling process.

3. When the rice has cooled, whip the cream with the sugar and vanilla extract until it forms soft peaks. Gently fold the whipped cream into the rice until it's evenly distributed; the result should have a light, fluffy texture. You can serve it immediately or cover and refrigerate it to chill completely.

4. When ready to serve, you can gently warm the cherry sauce if desired, or serve it chilled. Scoop individual portions of rice cream using an ice cream scoop or a large spoon. Spoon some cherry sauce over each portion of rice cream and serve immediately.

Short Grain Rice

Short grain rice cooks up plump and tender, and has a tendency to clump. It's often used in rice puddings and sushi. Since short, medium, and long grain rice behave differently when cooked, it's best to use the kind of rice called for in a given recipe, rather than attempt to substitute one type for another.

Know Your Ingredients

Dragon Fruit Sherbet

Dragon fruit is a truly international fruit. From its origin in Central and South America, it was introduced to Vietnam over 100 years ago, and it is now cultivated all over the world in tropical and subtropical climates. For this dragon fruit sherbet recipe, you can use the more common type of dragon fruit, which has white flesh—or you can seek out the less common type, which has bright fuschia flesh, for a dramatically colorful sherbet.

Prep Time: About 15 minutes
Inactive Time. 2 hours for chilling
    plus 1 hour for freezing
Total Time: 3 hours 15 minutes
Yield: 4 cups

1. Place the dragon fruit, honeydew melon, sugar, and vanilla in the bowl of a food processor fitted with a knife blade. Process until smooth and the sugar is dissolved.
2. Pour mixture into a bowl. Whisk in half and half. Chill thoroughly, at least 2 hours or overnight.
3. Pour chilled mixture into an ice cream maker and freeze according to the manufacturer's instructions.
4. Transfer sherbet to a freezer safe container. Freeze for at least one hour prior to serving to allow the sherbet to become firm.

2 cups chopped dragon fruit flesh
    (make sure the peel is completely
    removed; it is not edible)
1 cup chopped honeydew melon flesh
¾ cup sugar
1 teaspoon pure vanilla extract
1 cup half and half

Butter Pecan Applesauce Cake

Applesauce cake originates from the colonial era of the United States. It became even more popular when recipes for applesauce cake appeared in many American cookbooks during World War I. This gluten free version is topped with a decadent butter pecan sauce.

Prep Time: 15 minutes
Cook Time: 45 minutes
Total Time: 1 hour
Yield: 8 slices

For the cake:
2 cups gluten free flour blend
1 ½ teaspoon baking powder
½ teaspoon baking soda
½ teaspoon sea salt
3 teaspoons pumpkin pie spice
2 large eggs beaten
2 egg yolks beaten
1 cup unsweetened applesauce
1 cup sour cream
1 teaspoon vanilla
1 cup granulated sugar

For the butter pecan topping:
¼ cup light cream
¼ cup brown sugar
2 tablespoons brown sugar
2 tablespoons butter
½ cup pecans halves and pieces

For the cake:

1. Preheat the oven to 350°F. Prepare a 9 inch round cake pan by lining the bottom with a circle of parchment paper (use a smear of butter on the inside of the pan to make the paper stick if needed).

2. Combine the flour, baking powder, baking soda, salt, and pumpkin pie spice in a large mixing bowl. Whisk to combine. This is the "dry mix."

3. Combine the beaten eggs and yolks, applesauce, sour cream, vanilla, and sugar in a second mixing bowl. Beat until combined; liquid will look pale yellow and slightly foamy on top. This is the "liquid mix."

4. Stir the liquid mix into the dry mix, scraping down the sides of the bowl as needed, until just combined. Pour into the prepared pan.

5. Bake for 45 minutes, or until a toothpick / cake tester inserted in the center comes out clean. The cake will puff up a lot while baking; this is normal. When it's done, let it cool completely in the pan on a rack.

For the butter pecan topping:

1. Combine light cream, brown sugar, and butter in a small saucepan. Heat, stirring, until the sugar has dissolved. Add the pecans and bring to a boil for 2 minutes, stirring constantly, until slightly thickened. Let cool slightly. To serve, top each slice of cake with a spoonful or two of the topping.

Lemon Givré

Givré is a French word that means "frosted." It also refers to sorbet that is served in a frozen fruit peel. Each serving of lemon givré is elegantly presented in a frozen half of a lemon.

Prep Time: 5 minutes for the base
plus 20 minutes for processing
Inactive Time: 2 hours for chilling
plus 2 hours for freezing
Total Time: 4 hours 25 minutes
Yield: 3 cups (6 servings)

---

1 ½ cups water
1 cup sugar
Pinch of salt
1 cup fresh lemon juice (from approximately 6 to 8 large lemons)
Lemon zest, for serving (optional)

1. Juice the lemons until you have 1 cup of juice. Reserve 6 juiced lemon halves. Trim a small slice from the bottom tip of each lemon half to create a flat spot, so that it is easier for it to sit upright without tipping. Place the juiced lemon halves in the freezer.
2. Combine the water and sugar in a medium saucepan and cook over medium heat until sugar is completely dissolved. Remove from heat.
3. Add the lemon juice and salt, then stir to combine. Strain the mixture through a fine mesh strainer to remove any pulp, then cover and refrigerate for 2 hours, or overnight.
4. Process the mixture in an ice cream maker for 15 to 20 minutes until thickened. The sorbet will be soft. To make it firm, transfer to a container and freeze for at least 2 hours.
5. Scoop ½ cup of sorbet into each frozen lemon half. Garnish with additional lemon zest, if desired.

Variation:
To make a lemon basil sorbet, add ½ cup fresh basil leaves after step two and let steep for 30 minutes before continuing with step three. Garnish with a basil leaf in step five, if desired.

Raspberry Clafoutis

Clafoutis is a classic French dessert made by baking fruit in a thick custard. An equivalent amount of blueberries or pitted fresh cherries can be substituted for the raspberries.

Prep Time: 5 minutes
Cook Time: 30 minutes
Total Time: 35 minutes
Yield: 4 to 6 servings

1. Preheat oven to 400°F. Butter a 9-inch pie pan to prevent sticking.
2. Combine the flour, sugar, and salt in a mixing bowl. Whisk together. Add the eggs and whisk until smooth. Whisk in the vanilla and orange zest. Add the milk a little at a time, whisking after each addition until smooth.
3. Carefully pour the liquid into the pie pan. Place the raspberries evenly throughout the liquid.
4. Bake for 10 minutes at 400°F, then turn the temperature down to 350°F and continue baking for about 20 minutes, until the clafoutis is puffed up, the center is firm to the touch, and the outside edge has turned golden.
5. Place the pie pan on a rack to cool. Cool until just slightly warm, or room temperature. Garnish with powdered sugar just before serving.

2 teaspoons butter, or as much as is needed to butter the pan
½ cup gluten free flour blend
¼ cup granulated sugar
⅛ teaspoon salt
3 large eggs
1 tablespoon pure vanilla extract
1 cup milk
2 ½ cups raspberries, about 12 ounces
Powdered sugar, as needed, for garnish

Marsala Wine

Marsala is an Italian wine from the region of Sicily. Like sherry, it's a fortified wine, which means that extra spirits are added in at the end of the winemaking process to raise the alcohol content. Marsala can be sweet, semi-sweet, or dry (not sweet). Dry marsala is used in savory sauces, while sweet marsala is used in desserts such as zabaglione.

Nutmeg

Nutmeg is a sweet and powerfully aromatic spice that comes from the nutmeg tree. Primarily exported from the islands of Indonesia and Grenada, it can be purchased pre-ground, or as a whole seed. If purchased whole, the nutmeg seed can be grated on the smallest holes of a cheese grater to produce the freshest aroma and flavor. The spice called mace also comes from the nutmeg tree; it's the red covering (or "aril") of the nutmeg seed, which is removed, dried, and ground to create mace.

Know Your Ingredients

Zabaglione

Zabaglione is a whipped Italian custard flavored with Marsala wine. It can be served warm or cold along with fruit or cookies, and is especially pretty when served in a clear glass.

Prep Time: 5 minutes
Cook Time. 15 minutes
Total Time: 20 minutes*
Yield: 4 servings

*Add 2 hours if you wish to chill the zabaglione before serving.

---

1. Bring about 1 inch of water to a boil in a saucepan.
2. In a large heatproof bowl, add the egg yolks and sugar. Beat using an electric mixer on high speed until mixture is light and the sugar is dissolved, about 4 to 5 minutes. Scrape down the bowl during mixing to incorporate all the sugar.

6 egg yolks
½ cup sugar
⅔ cup sweet Marsala wine
Pinch of salt
⅛ teaspoon freshly grated nutmeg
1 teaspoon vanilla

3. Add the Marsala wine, salt and nutmeg to the bowl. Lower the heat to the saucepan to bring the water to a simmer. Place the bowl over the simmering water. Make sure the water is not touching the bottom of the bowl. Beat mixture on medium speed for about 13 minutes, until it is thick, about triple in volume, and registers 165°F on an instant-read thermometer. Remove bowl from pan. Add vanilla and beat to combine.
4. Serve immediately or chill completely before serving. Serve with fresh berries, gluten free cookies, or your favorite custard topping.

Shortbread Cookies

Traditional Scottish shortbread cookies are made with only five ingredients: gluten free oat flour, butter, vanilla, sugar, and salt. These gluten free shortbread cookies are just as pure and simple, with a buttery crunch and a tantalizing aroma. Measuring the ingredients by weight, rather than by volume, will help you get perfect results every time.

Prep Time: 15 minutes
Cook Time: 13 minutes
Total Time: 28 minutes
Yield: 30 cookies

2.75 ounces granulated sugar
5.25 ounces gluten free oat flour
¼ teaspoon sea salt or kosher salt
4 ounces salted butter room
    temperature, softened
1 teaspoon pure vanilla extract
1 tablespoon turbinado sugar,
    the kind with large individual
    crystals of sugar

1. Preheat the oven to 350°F. Line two baking sheets with parchment. Whisk together the sugar, flour, and salt in a large mixing bowl.
2. Add the butter to the mixing bowl and drizzle the vanilla over the butter. Mix with a fork (or "cut in") until a dough forms. Note: if the butter is a bit cold, the ingredients will not become a dough until you knead them together with your hands.
3. Roll out the dough to a thickness of ⅓ inch. Cut out rounds with a 1 ¾ inch cookie cutter. Note: if the dough is too soft to cut cleanly, refrigerate it for a 15 minutes or so until it firms up.
4. Place the rounds evenly and equally between the two baking sheets. Keep in mind that the cookies will spread slightly. Sprinkle turbinado sugar on top of each cookie round, then bake the cookies for 13 minutes.
5. Remove from oven and let cool completely. As soon as the cookies are completely cool, store them in an airtight container.

Turbinado Sugar

Oat flour is produced by grinding Unlike granulated sugar, which is refined to remove all of the molasses, turbinado sugar consists of less processed sugar crystals that retain much of the molasses extracted from the sugar cane. In addition, turbinado sugar crystals are much larger than granulated sugar crystals. Because of their large size, they're not as suitable for adding to batters and doughs, but they're perfect for adding a crunchy sugar garnish to a finished treat.

Know Your Ingredients

Ginger Matcha Ice Cream

This ice cream recipe combines matcha with fresh ginger to make a lovely green dessert that's creamy and refreshing.

Prep Time: 5 minutes
Inactive Time: 8 hours
Total Time: 8 hours 5 minutes
Yield: 3 cups

---

1 cup milk
¾ cup granulated sugar
1 tablespoon matcha powder
⅓ cup sliced fresh ginger (sliced into thin rounds like coins)
¼ teaspoon pure vanilla extract
Pinch cinnamon
2 cups heavy whipping cream

1. In a large mixing bowl, whisk together the milk, sugar, and matcha powder until the sugar is dissolved and the match powder is smoothly blended into the liquid.
2. Add the sliced ginger, vanilla, and cinnamon. Stir together until combined.
3. Add the heavy whipping cream and stir gently to combine.
4. Cover the bowl and let it sit in the refrigerator overnight.
5. Strain the mixture and process in an ice cream maker. Serve while soft, or freeze until firm.

POST MAIL
POST MAIL

Matcha

Matcha, or dried and powdered green tea, originated in China and was later brought to Japan. Ceremonial grade matcha is used in tea ceremonies, while lower grades of matcha are suitable for making casual cups of tea, or to flavor and color food.

Know Your Ingredients

Cinnamon

There are several varieties of cinnamon sold in grocery stores. The most frequently encountered variety is from the *Cinnamonum cassia* tree. Cassia cinnamon has a bold, spicy flavor, easily recognizable in cinnamon rolls and other baked goods. On the other hand, cinnamon from the *Cinnamonum verum* tree is known as Ceylon cinnamon or "true" cinnamon. True cinnamon has a floral aroma and a more delicate flavor than spicy cassia cinnamon, and for that reason, it's preferred for use in Mexican desserts.

Know Your Ingredients

Mexican Spiced Brownies

Mexican desserts often include Ceylon cinnamon, which is delicately fragrant, rather than the common variety of cassia cinnamon, which is more spicy. Mexican vanilla extract adds a subtle yet complex floral aroma.

Prep Time: 5 minutes
Cook Time: 25 minutes
Total Time: 30 minutes
Yield: 9 large brownies

1. Preheat the oven to 350°F and prepare an 8 inch square pan by lining it with parchment paper or foil.
2. In a small bowl, whisk together the cocoa powder, cinnamon, and red pepper. Set aside.
3. Place the sugar and the melted butter in a large mixing bowl and whisk together until combined. Add the eggs one at a time, whisking after each addition. Stir in the salt and the vanilla extract, then set aside the whisk.
4. Add the cocoa powder and spice mixture, then stir in gently with a spoon or spatula, making sure to scrape down the bowl as you go so that the mixture is fully incorporated.
5. Scrape the batter into the prepared pan and smooth out the top. Bake for 25 to 30 minutes, or until a toothpick inserted in the middle comes out with moist crumbs but no wet batter attached. Let cool in the pan for 15 minutes on a rack, then use the liner to lift out the brownies and set them on the rack to finish cooling.

1 ⅓ cups unsweetened cocoa powder
½ teaspoon Ceylon cinnamon (if you use regular cinnamon, reduce amount to ¼ teaspoon)
1 pinch ground red pepper
12 tablespoons unsalted butter, melted
1 ¼ cups granulated sugar
½ cup brown sugar
3 large eggs
¼ teaspoon salt
1 teaspoon Mexican vanilla extract (substitute any pure vanilla extract if needed)

Apple Crumble

Crumbles are a British dessert made by layering a crumbly topping over fruit. This gluten free apple crumble includes almond flour for extra nuttiness and texture. If you can make apple crumble, you can make just about any kind of fruit crumble you can imagine. Simply substitute 3 cups of blackberries, raspberries, or blueberries (or mixed berries) for the apple slices. To dress it up, garnish with whipped cream or vanilla ice cream.

Prep Time: 10 minutes
Cook Time: 30 minutes
Total Time: 40 minutes
Yield: 4 servings

2 apples, medium size
5 tablespoons unsalted butter, softened
½ cup brown sugar, lightly packed
½ cup gluten free old fashioned oats
¼ cup almond flour
¼ cup gluten free flour blend
¼ teaspoon cinnamon
⅛ teaspoon salt

1. Preheat the oven to 375°F and set out a 1 quart baking dish and a mixing bowl. If you wish to peel the apples, peel them now.
2. Cut the apples into 8 slices each, removing the core. Cut each slice into three short pieces to make apple chunks of approximately equal size. You'll need about 3 cups of apple chunks. Place the apple chunks in the 1 quart baking dish.
3. In a mixing bowl, whisk the sugar, oats, flours, cinnamon, and salt (if used) together. Add the butter and mix with a fork until the ingredients have formed into small clumps. Once the ingredients have clumped together, there should be no loose flour or sugar in the bowl and no visible bits of butter.
4. Using the back of the fork, compact the mixture firmly into the bowl until it sticks together in one large clump. Hold the clump in your hand over the the top of the apple chunks. Break off pieces of the clump and let them fall on top of the apples in chunks. It should cover the top relatively evenly.
5. Place the pan in the oven and bake for 30 minutes, or until the top is golden brown. Let cool until just slightly warm so that the topping can firm up before serving.

Oven Baked S'mores

The s'more is an American treat originally known as "Some More." The recipe was first published in 1927 in a Girl Scout guidebook called "Tramping and Trailing with the Girl Scouts." The original recipe requires a real campfire, but this version requires only an oven.

Prep Time: 1 minute
Cook Time: No more than 1 minute
Total Time: 2 minutes
Yield: Adjustable

---

1. Move an oven rack to a position about 6 inches from the broiler element at the top of the oven.
2. Turn on the broiler (on high, if you have a choice between low and high).
3. Prepare a baking sheet by lining it with foil fo easy cleanup,

Gluten free graham crackers
Large marshmallows
Chocolate bars

4. Place as many graham crackers as you want on the baking sheet.
5. Break or cut the chocolate into pieces that will fit on top of each graham cracker without hanging off. Place chocolate on each graham cracker, and a marshmallow (standing on its flat end) on top of each chocolate piece.
6. Slide the baking sheet on to the oven rack. Close the oven door and count to 10. Open the oven door and slide out baking sheet to check if the tops of the marshmallows are golden brown; if not, return them to the oven for another 10 seconds. The time it takes to brown the marshmallows will vary depending on how close they are to the broiler and whether it was preheated or not, so you will need to check every 10 seconds to make sure they don't burn.
7. Top each smore with another graham cracker and serve immediately, while warm.

Grape Molasses

Grape molasses is a thick, sweet syrup made from crushed grapes and juice. It's traditionally used in Turkish cuisine to flavor sweets, and is considered to be a nutritious addition due to its iron and potassium content.

Rose Water & Rose Petals

Rose water is made by steeping rose petals in water. It's used in Middle Eastern cuisine to flavor drinks, candy, and other sweet desserts. Edible dried rose petals can be used to garnish desserts as well. When you shop for dried rose petals, make sure they are marked as edible; you don't want to accidentally use potpourri in your food.

Know Your Ingredients

Carrot Halva

This orange confection is associated with the Iranian winter festival known as Shab-e Yalda, which is celebrated on the longest night of the year. Halva is dense, sweet, and can be served with bread, or alone as a fudge-like dessert.

Prep Time: 15 minutes
Cook Time: 40 minutes
Total Time: 55 minutes
Yield: 12 servings

1. Wash, peel, and grate the carrots. You may use a food processor on pulse to grate the carrots (do not purée). Place in a saucepan and add 2 cups water and the sugar. Bring to a boil stirring constantly until the sugar completely dissolves. Reduce heat to low, cover, and simmer for 30 minutes.
2. In a large Dutch oven, heat the oil over high heat and gradually add the rice flour while stirring constantly. Cook for 5 to 8 minutes or until the mixture turns lightly golden.
3. Reduce heat to low. Wear oven mitts and carefully add the cooked carrot to the hot rice flour (step back to avoid getting splashed). Add saffron-rose water and cardamom, and cook over low heat for another 15 to 20 minutes, stirring quickly and constantly with a wooden spoon to make a thick, smooth halva.
4. Place a ring on a flat serving platter and spoon the halva into it; pack firmly with a spoon. Garnish with ground pistachios, walnuts, rose petals and cinnamon. Allow to cool, lift up the ring, then cover and chill in the refrigerator.

2 pounds carrots
2 cups sugar or grape molasses
1 cup canola oil or unsalted butter
2 cups sifted rice flour
½ teaspoon ground saffron dissolved in ½ cup rose water
1 tablespoon ground cardamom
2 tablespoons ground pistachios
2 tablespoons ground walnuts
2 tablespoons dried rose petals, crushed
¼ teaspoon ground cinnamon

Recipe contributed by Najmieh Batmanglij, author of Food of Life: Ancient Persian and Modern Iranian Cooking and Ceremonies.

Pineapple Tarts

This traditional Chinese New Year snack features soft pastry surrounding a delicious, but not-too-sweet, pineapple filling. To save time, you can use pineapple jam instead of making pineapple filling from scratch, but the time it takes to make the filling yourself is well worth the result.

Prep Time: 30 minutes
Cook Time: 2 hours for the pineapple filling, 15 minutes for tart baking
Inactive Time: 1 hour for chilling the dough and allowing the filling to cool
Total Time: 3 hours 45 minutes
Yield: Varies

For the filling:
4 medium pineapples with outer skin and eyes removed (be sure to remove all the brown bits)

For the pastry:
2 cups gluten free flour blend (recommended brand: Bob's Red Mill Gluten Free 1-to-1 Baking Flour)
1 ¼ cups salted butter, frozen and cut into small pieces
2 eggs, beaten
Up to 3 tablespoons cold water

For assembly:
1 egg, beaten
1 tablespoon water

For the filling:

1. After cleaning your pineapples, chop by hand or use a food processor. You should still be able to see small chunks of pineapple.
2. Bring pineapple to a boil in a large heavy pan. Reduce the heat to medium and cook for several hours until the pulp turns brown and the moisture is mostly cooked out. If you prefer a slightly sweeter filling, add sugar to taste while pineapple cooks down.
3. Cool the filling and roll into balls. The size of the balls will depend on how you plan to shape your tarts.

For the pastry:

1. By hand or food processor, cut the butter into the flour until it is mixed in.
2. Add the eggs and 1 tablespoon of cold water at a time. Pulse to mix. As you pulse, the butter will melt and the dough will begin to stick to itself.
3. Chill the dough for 30 minutes to 1 hour. Cut off manageable pieces and roll out using gluten free flour on the surface to prevent sticking.

Assembly and Baking:

1. Begin preheating the oven to 350°F.
2. Whisk the beaten egg and water together to make an egg wash
3. Roll out dime-sized filling balls. Using cookie cutter, cut round circles and encase filling. You can use your fingers with a touch of water to close off the seams. As a finishing touch, stick a clove into the top. Brush with egg wash for extra shininess.
4. Roll out slightly larger filling balls. Using a cookie cutter, cut round circles and place them in oiled muffin cups. You can make the edges flat to the muffin tin or flowing like a skirt. Place the filling on top of the dough and fold over the top so the filling is almost covered. Brush with egg wash and sprinkle with cinnamon and sugar for added sweetness. Bake at 350°F for about 15 minutes, or until the pastry is just turning golden brown. Cool tarts on rack.

Recipe contributed by Kristine Miller of One Degree Gluten Free (https://onedegreeglutenfree.com) a source for information, recipes and building community among those who are eating gluten free in Singapore.

TECHNIQUE TAKEAWAY

Five More Ways to Flavor Whipped Cream

1. Substitute a pinch of ground nutmeg, ginger, or cardamom for the cinnamon.
2. Add a few drops (to taste) of pure extract, such as vanilla, rum, mint, or lemon.
3. Stir in a teaspoon of zest from an orange, lemon, or lime.
4. Add a tablespoon or so (to taste) of flavored liqueur, such as Amaretto, crème de cassis, Grand Marnier, or crème de menthe.
5. Try mixing and matching different flavors: vanilla plus cardamom, ginger plus lemon, or nutmeg plus orange zest and and rum.

Remember to wait until after the cream is whipped to soft peaks to gently fold in the flavorings, then continue whipping until the whipped cream makes stiff peaks.

Apple Parfait

Parfait is French for "perfect," which is an excellent description of this combination of tender sauteed apples, crunchy granola, and delicately flavored whipped cream. It's equally good for breakfast, snack, or a late night treat.

Prep Time: 15 minutes
Cook Time: 40 minutes
Total Time: 55 minutes
Yield: 12 servings

---

1. Place a mixing bowl and whisk in the refrigerator to chill.
2. Heat a nonstick skillet on medium low. Drop in the butter and let it melt and bubble gently. If it sizzles audibly, the skillet is too hot.
3. Add the apple slices and toss to coat. Sprinkle on the brown sugar and toss again. Let cook, stirring and turning the slices occasionally, for about 10 to 15 minutes. Apples are done when they are easily pierced by a fork. Remove the skillet from heat and set aside.
4. Remove the chilled bowl and whisk. Add the whipped cream and whisk briskly until soft peaks are formed. Add the cinnamon and keep whisking until cinnamon is completely incorporated.
5. Divide the apple slices between 4 serving dishes. Divide granola equally between the 4 serving dishes, then top with a dollop of cinnamon whipped cream. Serve immediately.

2 medium apples cored and sliced
    (recommended: Honeycrisp or Pink
    Lady / Cripps Pink)
1 tablespoon unsalted butter
1 tablespoon lemon juice
1 teaspoon brown sugar
½ cup heavy whipping cream
Pinch of cinnamon
1 cup gluten free granola

Raw Hamantaschen with Chocolate Filling

Hamantaschen are triangle-shaped cookies with filling in the middle. They are traditionally made to celebrate Purim, the joyous Jewish holiday that commemorates how Queen Esther saved the Jews of ancient Persia. This no-bake version of hamantaschen is simple and fast.

Prep Time: 15 minutes
Cook Time: 0 minutes
Total Time: 15 minutes
Yield: 8 cookies

For the filling:
¼ cup raw nut butter of choice
2 tablespoons raw cacao powder
1 tablespoon raw honey

For the hamantaschen:
⅔ cup raw pecans
⅓ cup shredded unsweetened coconut
¼ teaspoon cinnamon
Pinch of salt
12 medjool dates, pitted
    (about 1 cup pitted dates)

Recipe contributed by Alana Horowitz Friedman, food blogger and recipe developer at www. thesmilingonion.com.

For the filling:
1. Place the nut butter in a small bowl. Add the cacao and honey and mix until a smooth consistency is reached.

For the hamantaschen:
2. Place the pecans, coconut, cinnamon, and salt in the bowl of your food processor. Pulse the mixture several times, until it resembles coarse crumbs. Add the dates and pulse several more times, until the mixture becomes a sticky dough.
3. Form the hamantaschen by dividing the dough into 8 equal parts. For each cookie, pinch the sides of the dough so that a triangle with an indentation in the middle is formed. Fill with your choice of filling(s), then enjoy as is or place in the fridge to harden slightly. Store the cookies in an airtight container in the fridge. They can also be frozen.

Raw Cacao Powder

Raw cacao powder and cocoa powder may look the same, but there's one major difference: cocoa powder is heated to a high temperature during processing, while raw cacao powder is not. This means that raw cacao powder is less processed and contains greater quantities of healthful antioxidants. Raw cacao powder is commonly used in "raw," or uncooked, recipes instead of cocoa powder.

Natural cocoa powder and raw cacao powder can usually be substituted for one another, but (depending on the recipe) raw cacao powder is not always interchangeable with Dutch processed cocoa powder. Dutch processed cocoa powder is treated with alkali and behaves differently in the presence of other baking ingredients such as baking powder and baking soda.

Know Your Ingredients

Vietnamese Coffee

You can pick up a Vietnamese coffee filter set at an Asian grocery store or online for about $10, and it's well worth it for the fun of watching the coffee brew. Use a clear glass coffee mug so you can watch the coffee drip and swirl into the layer of sweetened condensed milk at the bottom of the mug. You can drink it hot, or you can pour the mixture directly over a tall glass of ice to make iced Vietnamese coffee.

Prep Time: 1 minute
Cook Time: 4 minutes
Total Time: 5 minutes
Yield: 1 serving

3 tablespoons Vietnamese coffee, or 20 grams (recommended brand: Trung Nguyen, or substitute Cafe Du Monde)
2 tablespoons sweetened condensed milk

1. Place the coffee mug on a flat surface. Pour in enough sweetened condensed milk to make a layer on the bottom of the cup.
2. Top with the dish-like section of the filter.
3. Place the cup section of the filter on top of that. Measure out about 3 tablespoons of coffee (20 grams) and place in the filter cup.
4. Put the filter insert on top of the coffee.
5. Tap it down very gently and spin it a few times to level the coffee grounds.
6. Add just a little very hot, but not boiling, water to the filter; it should be just enough to moisten the coffee grounds. Wait 20 seconds for the water to soak in.
7. Add enough water to almost fill up the coffee filter cup. Cover with the lid and let brew for a maximum of 4 minutes.
8. Remove the entire filter set (it will drip; have an extra mug handy that you can put it on).
9. Stir the sweetened condensed milk into the coffee. Serve hot or pour over ice.

Vietnamese Coffee

Vietnamese coffee can be made from several types of coffee beans, such as the Arabica, Robusta, and Excelsa varieties, and it's typically dark roasted. Because it often contains Robusta beans, which have much more caffeine than Arabica beans, Vietnamese coffee is particularly energizing.

Trung Nguyen is the biggest coffee producer in Vietnam and the most widely available Vietnamese coffee brand available in the United States. Cafe du Monde coffee (from New Orleans) has also been adopted for brewing Vietnamese-style coffee in the United States.

Know Your Ingredients

Chai Hot Cocoa

Chai spices may be familiar to you from chai tea, but they're just as good when added to homemade hot cocoa. You can adjust the level of spice to your taste, or adjust the amount of milk to make the cocoa stronger or lighter.

Prep Time: 0 minutes
Cook Time: 5 minutes
Total Time: 5 minutes
Yield: 2 servings

⅓ cup water
⅓ cup unsweetened cocoa powder
⅓ cup sugar
2 green cardamom pods, cracked open
4 black peppercorns
2 pieces star anise
1 slice fresh ginger
Pinch of cinnamon
1 ½ cups milk or more

1. In a small saucepan, combine all of the ingredients except the milk. Whisk briskly to combine.
2. Heat the mixture until steaming hot over medium heat (do not boil) and whisk briskly for a minute or two until the sugar is dissolved and mixture is glossy and dark-colored.
3. Slowly whisk in the milk until frothy and slightly steamy, but do not let it boil. Taste, and add more milk if desired. Strain into mugs and serve.

Cardamom

Cardamom is an intensely flavored spice that originated in India. It's considered the third most expensive spice in the world (after saffron and vanilla), and is used in both sweet and savory dishes. Because it loses much of its flavor after being ground, it's best to buy whole cardamom pods and then grind the spice as needed.

The most commonly used type of cardamom is green (or "true") cardamom. Green cardamom pods can be cracked open under the flat of a knife or by lightly crushing them with a pestle; then the black seeds can be removed and ground (if desired), or used whole. In the accompanying chai hot cocoa recipe, there's no need to pick out the seeds. They'll be strained out along with the cracked pod.

Star Anise

Star anise has a licorice-like flavor and, although it tastes similar to anise, it is not botanically related. Star anise can be ground, as it is used in Chinese five spice powder, or used whole, as in this chai hot cocoa recipe. It can also be used to flavor mulled wine, liquor, and coffee.

Know Your Ingredients

Recommended Reading

Down South Paleo by Jennifer Robins. A completely gluten free take on Southern American cuisine, Down South Paleo shows you how to make Southern foods like fried chicken, squash casserole, hushpuppies, and pecan pie. Each recipe is marked to indicate for which allergies it's suitable (i.e. dairy-free, nut-free, etc.), making it ideal for households with multiple sensitivities.

The Gloriously Gluten-Free Cookbook by Vanessa Maltin. This cookbook is split into three sections: Italian, Asian, and Mexican. Each section contains recipes for creating gluten free meals using each cuisine's signature ingredients and techniques, plus shopping advice for filling your pantry with the necessary ingredients.

Gluten-Free Artisan Bread in Five Minutes a Day by Jeff Hertzberg and Zoë François. From just one "Master Recipe," you can create boules, baguettes, ciabatta, and more. This detailed bread-baking cookbook also provides instructions for other bread varieties, such as pizza, naan, and pastries, using the Master Recipe or other variations that utilize one of the two gluten free flour mix recipes provided.

The Gluten-Free Asian Kitchen by Laura B. Russell. If you've ever despaired of being unable to enjoy Asian cuisine because of gluten, this is the cookbook for you. It contains recipes for noodles, dumplings, sauces, meats, seafood, vegetables, and more, all gluten free and carefully explained in highly detailed instructions.

The Gluten Free Italian Vegetarian Kitchen by Donna Klein. Meat-free, wheat-free, and gluten free, this cookbook is packed with over 225 recipes that cover appetizers, soups, salads, breads, pizza, and sandwiches, main dishes, side dishes, brunch, and dessert. Each recipe is also marked to indicate whether it's vegan, egg-free, dairy-free, lacto/ovo, or low-carb, in addition to being gluten and meat free.

Gluten Free on a Shoestring by Nicole Hunn. Although not specifically marketed as an international cookbook, this money-saving gluten free cookbook contains a variety of recipes that are inspired by cuisines from around the world. Within its pages, you'll find recipes like gnocchi, matzo ball soup, lo mein, profiteroles, and Szechuan meatballs, to name just a few, plus many American desserts.

The Gluten-Free Table by Jilly Lagasse and Jessie Lagasse Swanson. Co-authored by two daughters of Emeril Lagasse, this eclectic cookbook has a little bit of this and a little bit of that. It contains Italian recipes like Zucchini and Polenta Fritters, classic American dishes such as Waldorf Salad, Cajun recipes like Cheesy Shrimp and Crab Grits, and a handful of Asian-inspired recipes.

Latin American Paleo Cooking by Amanda Torres and Milagros Torres. Featuring traditional Latin American comfort foods made free of gluten, dairy, and refined sugar, this cookbook was inspired by the cuisine of Puerto Rico, Colombia, Cuba, and Venezuela. Savory dishes, like arepas, mofongo, and ropa vieja, take center stage, while naturally sweetened desserts, such as flan de coco, round off the meals.

The New Yiddish Kitchen by Jennifer Robins and Simone Miller. This cookbook presents a hearty serving of appetizers and soups, bread and crackers, condiments, deli favorites, main courses, salads and vegetables, plus a bevy of naturally sweetened desserts. To top it all off, there are homespun tips from "Bubbe" included throughout the book.

Nosh on This by Lisa Stander-Horel and Tim Horel. You know you're in for something good when the back cover says, "No cookie, strudel, brownie, pie, cake, tart, or treat left behind." This volume of Jewish-American sweets (plus a handful of savory items) has recipes for rugelach, donuts, challah, mandelbrot, and many other favorites.

Pâtisserie Gluten Free by Patricia Austin. Delectable French pastries are no longer off limits when you dive into this cookbook. Within its pages, you'll find precise ingredient weights, detailed instructions, and carefully chosen product recommendations so that you can create cookies, tarts, cakes, and puff pastries just like your favorite French bakery, except that they're completely gluten free.

Silk Road Vegetarian by Dahlia Abraham-Klein. Filled with flavorful, healthful recipes inspired by the ancient Silk Road of Asia, this cookbook focuses on richly spiced Central Asian cuisine, including (but not limited to) Afghan, Persian, and Indian food. It's packed with plenty of helpful tips on preparation and cooking procedures.

Trés Green Trés Clean Trés Chic by Rebecca Leffler. If French food makes you say "Oui!," you'll enjoy this volume of healthy gluten free and plant-based recipes with a French twist. In addition to the recipes, it also includes a section that teaches you techniques for creating recipe elements like plant-based milk, yogurt, butter and cheese.

Contributors

Liz Alvarez is the founder, writer, and wildly creative cook at Building Our Rez (BuildingOur-Rez.com). Mother-blogger (watch your mouth). Frugal Foodie. Never measured an ingredient in her life. Modern Minimalist. Hospitalitizer. The plan executor. The design eye. The sweet & salty, sugar & spice, fire & ice, no fuss, no frills, put your big girl panties on and take it like a woman. Achiever. Winner. The inclusivist. Your fierce advocate. Best friend to many. True to all.

Caleb Backe is a personal trainer as well as an expert in health and wellness for MapleHolistics, a company dedicated to cruelty-free and natural personal care products. Growing up a passionate foodie and fitness maven, Caleb has been able to pursue both his professional and leisurely passions by working with MapleHolistics on becoming a leader in e-commerce.

Najmieh Batmanglij has spent the past 39 years cooking, traveling, and adapting authentic Persian recipes to tastes and techniques in the West. She has been hailed as "the guru of Persian cuisine" by The Washington Post. Her *Food of Life* was called "the definitive book on Iranian cooking" by the Los Angeles Times. Her *Silk Road Cooking* was selected as one of the 10 best vegetarian cookbooks of 2004 by The New York Times; and her book *From Persia to Napa: Wine at the Persian Table* won the Gourmand Cookbook Award for the best wine history book of 2007. Najmieh is a member of Les Dames d'Escoffier and lives in Washington, DC, where she teaches Persian cooking, and consults with restaurants around the world.

Scott Burgett, founder of PlantBasedScotty.com, is a vegan food blogger living in Austin, TX. In January 2017, after learning about all the great benefits of eating vegan, he switched cold turkey and has never looked back. He now writes about staying healthy on a vegan diet and whips up delicious recipes for you to enjoy. When he's not in the kitchen, you can find him on a trail or the gym and spending time with his wife and dog.

Renee Dobbs is a self-proclaimed Domestic Goddess who loves to eat, drink, and dig in the dirt. She is enjoying life in the South and experiencing flavors from around the world. Cooking will always be one of her passions along with gardening and spoiling her whippets. You can read more of her food adventures on Magnolia Days, a blog she created and filled with recipes until retiring from it in 2017.

Alana Horowitz Friedman is a gluten-free food blogger and recipe developer at www.thesmilingonion.com and a personal chef in the New York area. A graduate of the Natural Gourmet Institute and lifelong vegetarian, her recipes are inspired by cuisines from around the world, and she specializes in crafting dishes for a wide variety of dietary preferences. Alana currently lives in Weehawken, NJ with her husband and their beloved cat, Sashimi.

Kristine Miller loves to adapt delicious recipes to fit her family's gluten-free requirements. While living in Southeast Asia, Kristine discovered the joy and challenge of creating local cuisine without using wheat-based soy sauce and other gluten-filled ingredients. Kristine especially loves cooking Vietnamese and Thai food because of its fresh ingredients and combination of sweet, salty, spicy, and umami.

National Pasta Association (NPA) is the leading trade association for the U.S. pasta industry. The association provides leadership to the industry on public policy issues, serving as its voice in Washington, D.C. NPA also forges alliances with key organizations, monitors and addresses technical issues and conducts nutrition and food safety research on behalf of the U.S. pasta industry.

Kati Schmidt is passionate about immigration, female founders, and gluten free food. She co-founded glutenfreiheit.org, Germany's #1 portal focusing on celiac disease and the gluten free lifestyle, after being diagnosed with celiac disease in 2010. In April 2018, she started a new venture, Piña Colada, connecting groups of six like-minded singles over great—and upon request gluten free—food in San Francisco's best restaurants.

Spices, Inc. is a leading online resource for all things educational and product related in the realm of herbs, spices, chiles, and seasoning blends. In addition to their inventory of more than 500 products, their recipes are developed by their in-house chef to inspire and challenge cooks of all skill levels to bring more flavor and better ingredients to the kitchen table.

Recipe Index

Know Your Ingredients Index

Sidebars with in-depth information on specific ingredients.

Technique Takeaway Index

Helpful kitchen techniques and bonus recipe variations.

About the Author

KATIE MOSEMAN is the author of *Fixin' to Eat: Southern Cooking for the Southern at Heart*, *I Hate Vegetables Cookbook: Fresh and Easy Vegetable Recipes That Will Change Your Mind*, and *Gluten Free World Tour Cookbook: Internationally Inspired Gluten Free Recipes*. She is a writer, photographer, and recipe developer whose work can be found on her blogs, Recipe for Perfection and Magnolia Days, as well as in numerous national publications. She lives in Florida with her husband and two children.

Made in United States
Troutdale, OR
12/19/2024

26932563R00066